AMERICAN HISTORY

The Cold War

Richard Brownell

LUCENT BOOKS
A part of Gale, Cengage Learning

GALE
CENGAGE Learning™

Detroit • New York • San Francisco • New Haven, Conn • Waterville, Maine • London

LIBRARY OF CONGRESS CATALOGING-IN-PUBLICATION DATA

Brownell, Richard.
  The Cold War / by Richard Brownell.
     p. cm. — (American history)
  Includes bibliographical references and index.
  ISBN 978-1-4205-0032-5 (hbk.)
  1. Cold War—Juvenile literature. I. Title.
  D843.B743 2009
  909.82'5—dc22

                                                        2008026589

Lucent Books
27500 Drake Rd.
Farmington Hills, MI 48331

ISBN-13: 978-1-4205-0032-5
ISBN-10: 1-4205-0032-5

Printed in the United States of America
2 3 4 5 6 7 12 11 10 09

Contents

Foreword   5
Important Dates at the Time of the Cold War   6

Introduction:
One War Leads to Another   8

Chapter One:
The Iron Curtain   12

Chapter Two:
New Commitments, New Dangers   25

Chapter Three:
The Cold War Goes Global   37

Chapter Four:
The Success and Failure of Flexible Response   49

Chapter Five:
A New Approach   61

Chapter Six:
Taking on the Evil Empire   72

Chapter Seven:
The Fall of the Soviet Union   84

Notes   94
Glossary   97
For Further Exploration   98
Index   100
Picture Credits   104
About the Author   104

Foreword

The United States has existed as a nation for just over 200 years. By comparison, Rome existed as a nation-state for more than 1,000 years. Out of a few struggling British colonies, the United States developed relatively quickly into a world power whose policy decisions and culture have great influence on the world stage. What events and aspirations drove this young American nation to such great heights in such a short period of time? The answer lies in a close study of its varied and unique history. As James Baldwin once remarked, "American history is longer, larger, more various, more beautiful, and more terrible than anything anyone has ever said about it."

The basic facts of United States history—names, dates, places, battles, treaties, speeches, and acts of Congress—fill countless textbooks. These facts, though essential to a thorough understanding of world events, are rarely compelling for students. More compelling are the stories in history, the experience of history.

Titles in this series explore the history of the country and the experiences of Americans. What influences led the colonists to risk everything and break from Britain? Who was the driving force behind the Constitution? Which factors led thousands of people to leave their homelands and settle in the United States? Questions like these do not have simple answers; by discussing them, however, we can view the past as a more real, interesting, and accessible place.

Students will find excellent tools for research and investigation in every title. Lucent Books' American History series provides not only facts, but also the analysis and context necessary for insightful critical thinking about history and about current events. Fully cited quotations from historical figures, eyewitnesses, letters, speeches, and writings bring vibrancy and authority to the text. Annotated bibliographies allow students to evaluate and locate sources for further investigation. Sidebars highlight important and interesting figures, events, or related primary source excerpts. Timelines, maps, and full-color images add another dimension of accessibility to the stories being told.

It has been said the past has a history of repeating itself, for good and ill. In these pages, students will learn a bit about both and, perhaps, better understand their own place in this world.

Important Dates at the Time

1945
World War II
ends on
September 2
with the formal
surrender of
Japan.

1947
On April 11
Jackie Robinson
joins the Brook-
lyn Dodgers,
breaking the
color barrier in
Major League
Baseball.

1948
The Marshall
Plan is signed
into law on
April 3,
providing a
massive
economic aid
package to
rebuild war-
torn Europe. On
June 24 the
Soviets
blockade Berlin.

1956
Egypt nationalizes the
Suez Canal on July 26.
Britain, France, and Israel
invade the Sinai
Peninsula. The United
States forces a settlement,
and the Canal Zone is
placed under the
management of the
United Nations.

| 1940 | 1945 | 1950 | 1955 | 1960 | 1965 |

1957
The Soviet satellite
Sputnik is launched on
October 4, forcing
America to double its
efforts to develop a
superior space
program.

1962
On October 16
the discovery of
Soviet missiles in
Cuba by the
United States
leads to a tense
standoff,
bringing
America and the
USSR to the
brink of nuclear
war.

1963
On August 28
Martin Luther
King Jr. delivers
his "I Have a
Dream" speech
in Washington,
D.C.

1967
Thurgood
Marshall is
sworn in as the
first black
Supreme Court
justice on
October 2.

of the Cold War

1969
Americans land on the Moon on July 20.

1973
Peace accords end the Vietnam War on January 27; South Vietnam falls to the Communists two years later.

1979
A partial meltdown occurs at the Three Mile Island nuclear reactor in Pennsylvania on March 28.

1970   **1975**   **1980**   **1985**   **1990**   **1995**

1984
Reagan is reelected on November 6, carrying forty-nine states and 525 electoral votes.

1988
On December 7 Gorbachev announces large cuts in Soviet armed forces and military equipment.

1989
East German citizens in Berlin overrun the border to be reunited with family members on November 9; within a year, the Berlin Wall is completely torn down.

1991
Kuwait is liberated on February 27 after a massive U.S.-led international force decimates the Iraqi armed forces.

Introduction

One War Leads to Another

"With the defeat of the Reich . . . there will remain in the world only two Great Powers capable of confronting each other—the United States and Soviet Russia."

—Adolf Hitler, quoted in *The Testament of Adolf Hitler (February–April 1945)*, edited by François Genoud

In 1941 the United States of America and the Soviet Union possessed views of the world so distinct that each nation saw the other as a threat to its own existence and to the world as a whole. America was a democracy in which the citizens freely elected their leaders and open political discourse was considered essential to liberty. America's economic system was free-market capitalism, in which the means of production were owned by private individuals and corporations that reaped the profits of their labor and the price of goods was set by their demand in the marketplace.

The Soviet Union, officially known as the Union of Soviet Socialist Republics (USSR), embraced the economic system of communism that, in theory, meant that the workers owned the means of production and the profits were shared equally by everyone. In reality, the Soviet Union was a dictatorship in which the government controlled everything. Citizens could vote for their leaders, but all political parties except for the Communist Party were outlawed. Joseph Stalin, the ruler of the Soviet Union since 1929, had no tolerance for dissent. He ordered the imprisonment and execution of millions of party officials, military officers, and Soviet citizens who he believed held subversive political views.

Communists in the Soviet Union and abroad wanted to overthrow the free-market nations of the world because they believed capitalism enslaved workers to make the rich richer. America and other free-market nations wanted to prevent the spread of communism because they recognized that it meant an end to individual freedom of choice and democracy. These fundamental disagreements between the two nations were put aside during World War II, however, because both nations were threatened by Nazi Germany.

Allies

American president Franklin D. Roosevelt and British prime minister Winston Churchill did not trust Stalin because of his adherence to the Communist ideology and his previously friendly dealings with Nazi leader Adolf Hitler.

After the Nazis invaded Russia on June 22, 1941, Roosevelt and Churchill recognized that they shared with Stalin the common goal of Hitler's defeat. They also knew it would take the combined might of the three nations to destroy the Nazis. Churchill explained the unexpected alliance to his secretary: "If Hitler invaded Hell, I would at least make a favorable mention of the Devil in the House of Commons."[1]

During the week of February 4 through 11, 1945, with the defeat of the Nazis finally in sight, Roosevelt, Churchill, and Stalin met in the city of Yalta in the Soviet Crimea to discuss the administration of

British prime minister Winston Churchill (left), President Franklin Roosevelt (center), and Soviet leader Joseph Stalin (right) meet at the Yalta conference in February 1945.

postwar Europe. They decided that Germany and the capital of Berlin would be divided into four occupation zones, with each nation and France governing a zone. The creation of the United Nations was proposed as a way for nations to peacefully settle disputes. The Soviet Union agreed to join the United States and Britain in the war against imperial Japan in Asia after Germany was defeated.

Strains in the alliance began to show when Stalin expressed his desire for a free hand in the affairs of the nations of Eastern Europe. More than 26 million Soviet citizens were killed during the war with the Nazis, and he was adamant about establishing a series of friendly states between Russia and Germany to prevent the possibility of such a horror ever happening again. Roosevelt accommodated this request after drawing a vague promise from Stalin to allow free elections in the countries in question, even though his senior advisers were deeply suspicious of Stalin. "There was no time when the danger from the Soviet Union was not a topic of anxious conversation among officers of the State Department," recalled Louis Halle, a member of the White House Policy Planning Staff. "And by the winter of 1944–5, as the day of victory approached, it became the predominant theme in Washington."[2]

Roosevelt died on April 12, and some historians have suggested that his ill health at Yalta allowed Stalin to push a tougher bargaining position than the American president would have otherwise accepted. Another view of Roosevelt's agreement to Stalin's involvement in Eastern Europe indicates that he may have overestimated his ability to influence the Soviet leader. History professor Ronald E. Powaski writes in his book, *The Cold War: The United States and the Soviet Union, 1917–1991*, Roosevelt's "attempt to accommodate the Soviet Union's security concerns undoubtedly gave Stalin the impression that Soviet occupation of Eastern Europe was acceptable to the United States."[3]

Enemies

The next meeting between the leaders of the United States, Great Britain, and the USSR took place in the German city of Potsdam from July 17 to August 2, 1945. By this point, Germany had surrendered and the postwar occupation had begun. Churchill had been voted out of office, and Clement Attlee was the new prime minister. Harry S. Truman was now president of the United States.

In the months since Yalta, Soviet troops and secret police in Poland, Bulgaria, and Romania had supported the local Communist parties in their attempts to seize power through military coups and rigged elections. Truman's advisers believed this was just the beginning of a Soviet attempt to bring all of Eastern Europe under its control, and Truman recognized that the Soviets needed to be dealt with more sternly than in the past. Truman realized that Germany may be needed in the future to serve as a buffer against Soviet expansion, so he refused to accept the Soviet demand for harsh reparations on Germany and the complete dismantling of its industrial infrastructure.

During the Potsdam conference, Truman received word about the successful

Delegates representing the United States, Great Britain, and the Soviet Union convene in Potsdam, Germany, in July 1945 to further outline the structure of postwar Europe.

test of the atomic bomb in the New Mexico desert. He suggested to Stalin that the United States was now in possession of a new weapon that could bring the war against Japan to a swift end. Stalin already knew of the bomb's existence because of spies in America's atomic research program. He ordered Soviet scientists to double their efforts to create their own weapon.

On August 6 and 9, 1945, the United States dropped two atomic bombs on Japan, forcing the surrender of imperial Japan and the end of World War II. Americans rejoiced at their victory over the forces of totalitarianism and looked forward to a new era of peace. In the Soviet capital of Moscow, Stalin also celebrated, but his outlook was different. "The First World War tore [Russia] away from capitalist slavery," Stalin told Foreign Minister Vyacheslav Molotov. "The Second World War created the socialist system, and the Third World War will finish [capitalism] forever."[4]

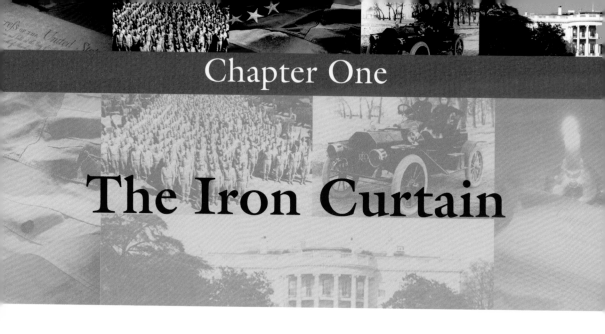

Chapter One

The Iron Curtain

"From Stettin in the Baltic to Trieste in the Adriatic, an iron curtain has descended across the Continent."
—Winston Churchill, March 5, 1946

The new international order that was created out of the ashes of World War II was shaped by the long-term goals of the victors, but those goals were in direct conflict with one another. The United States wanted to expand economic prosperity through the preservation of open markets and democratically elected governments. The Soviet Union wanted to secure its European border with a buffer zone of loyal satellite states and to continue to spread international communism through any means necessary. Europe quickly became an area of contention between the two countries as they each sought to rebuild in their own image a continent devastated by war.

The United States was uniquely suited as a global power to achieve its international goals, but there was debate about how best to deal with the Soviets. Stalin was not intimidated by American might or its possession of the atomic bomb, and he was deeply committed to expanding the political and military reach of the Soviet Union. By 1947 much of Eastern Europe had fallen under Communist control, and Western European leaders feared that their own nations were next on Stalin's list.

Stalin frequently resorted to diplomatic and military pressure to test just how far the United States would go in defense of its interests. American citizens did not want to go back to war, but leaders knew that if they did not stand up to the Soviets, communism would spread across Europe.

America at the Height of Power

The United States emerged from World War II as the world's most powerful nation. It had suffered just over four hundred thousand combat deaths in four years of fighting, or 0.32 percent of its population. Its great distance from Asia and Europe kept the country free from domestic attack by the enemy, and it was the only major industrialized nation with a manufacturing base that was running at full capacity in 1945. In fact, in that year the United States accounted for 25 percent of the gross domestic product for the entire world. This was greater than the production of all goods and services of Great Britain, the Soviet Union, France, and China combined.

Confidence among Americans was very high. Four long years of war had given way to a booming economy and widespread opportunities never before experienced. Home ownership, college education, and domestic comforts like washers, dryers, and refrigerators, previously enjoyed only by the wealthy, were now available to many Americans.

America's wartime allies were not so fortunate. The Soviet Union suffered more than 26 million deaths, or 13 percent of its population. The Nazi invasion, which reached the cities of Moscow and

Following World War II, the nations of Eastern Europe quickly fell under the control of the Soviet Union, while Western Europe was aligned with the interests of the United States, thus making the continent a key area of contention throughout the Cold War.

Stalingrad, resulted in the execution of millions of civilians and the disruption of Russia's industrial modernization.

Great Britain lost 450,000 people in the war, mostly in combat, but it paid a high price economically. Britain had been fighting the Nazis for close to two years before the United States and the Soviet Union joined the fighting. The bombardment of the British Isles and the attacks on its vast colonial holdings left it significantly weakened overseas. Military historian Norman Friedman notes in his book *The Fifty-Year War: Conflict and Strategy in the Cold War*, "World War II had cost Britain about a quarter of her prewar wealth, and left her the world's largest debtor."[5]

Britain's reduced power left a void that the United States needed to fill to prevent the Soviet Union from expanding its reach in Europe and overseas. Many Americans were wary of getting involved in foreign affairs, but times had changed. The country's new status as the preeminent global power gave it new responsibilities that it could not ignore without inviting international chaos. It also needed to ensure a stable international order for its growing business and economic interests.

A New Europe

America's commitment to protecting Europe began with rebuilding it, and that proved to be a daunting task. John McCloy, aide to Secretary of War Henry Stimson during World War II, visited Europe at the end of the war to assess the devastation. He reported to President

In 1945 German women clear rubble at the border between the British and American sectors of Berlin, which, like many areas of Europe, required extensive reconstruction after the devastation of World War II.

Truman, "There is complete economic, social, and political collapse going on in central Europe, the extent of which is unparalleled in history unless one goes back to the collapse of the Roman Empire."[6]

Germany also presented a unique challenge. The nation had been divided into four zones, but the United States quickly assumed responsibility for the French and British sectors because those governments could not afford the costs associated with extended occupation. Berlin, which was 110 miles (177km) inside the Soviet sector, was also divided into occupation zones, with the United States responsible for the western half of the bombed-out city, and the USSR responsible for the eastern half.

U.S. and Soviet negotiators had very different views about what should be done with postwar Germany. America wanted open elections throughout the country with the establishment of a free-market economy in part because it recognized that Communist infiltration proved successful in nations that were poor and had weak central governments. communism's practice of redistributing land and wealth appealed to the poor, despite the fact that they were often no better off after their nations turned to communism. Also, weak nondemocratic governments were easily corrupted and overthrown in favor of Communist regimes. Germany, like many of the nations of war-torn Europe, met both of these conditions.

The Soviets were against America's reconstruction strategy. Stalin believed that re-creating Germany in such a manner would swing the balance of power in Europe unfairly in the direction of the United States. He used this fear of American dominance over Europe to justify the Communist takeovers in Poland, Bulgaria, Romania, Yugoslavia, and the Baltic states of Latvia, Lithuania, and Estonia. It was also the motivation behind the Soviet desire to get America out of Germany altogether. In 1946 the Soviets began blocking shipments of agricultural products from their sector to the Western zones and installed people loyal to Moscow in the Berlin police force and municipal government.

The Communists were also expanding their presence in other European countries, becoming the largest political party in both France and Italy in 1946. The Communists claimed to offer a new direction from the existing political parties that had been in power when the war began. U.S. leaders knew that these political parties were taking their direction from Moscow. They were also aware of the Soviet hypocrisy regarding the governing of nations. Democratic governments were willing to allow the Communist Party to exist and support candidates for public office in Western European countries, but in the Soviet satellite countries of Eastern Europe, all political parties except the Communists were outlawed.

Former British prime minister Winston Churchill referred to Communist Eastern Europe as an iron curtain, behind which free nations were falling under the control of Moscow. It was a startling image that uniquely described the nature

George Kennan: The Architect of Containment

George Kennan was a member of America's diplomatic corps all his adult life. He was part of the first U.S. embassy staff in Moscow after formal relations were established with the Soviet Union in 1933. Kennan spent many years in Europe during the 1930s and 1940s, becoming an expert on Soviet behavior. In 1946 he wrote a 5,540-word cable that came to be known as "the Long Telegram," which warned of Stalin's expansionist foreign policy and became the basis for America's response.

Mark Feeney of the Boston Globe *explains:*

At that moment, its warnings about Soviet expansionism had an enormous impact, and for the next three years Mr. Kennan would be at the center of State Department decision-making: first as director of the department's Policy Planning Staff under Secretary George C. Marshall, in which capacity he played a key role in drafting the Marshall Plan, offering economic assistance to Western Europe; and then as counselor to Marshall's successor, Dean Acheson.

Kennan later spoke out against America's foreign policy in dealing with the Communists, believing that the country's actions led to decades of tension and billions of wasted dollars. He remained active in scholarly pursuits until his death in 2005 at the age of 101, and he is one of the most respected diplomats in American history.

Mark Feeney, "George Kennan Dies at 101; Devised Cold War Policy," *Boston Globe*, March 18, 2005.

American diplomat George Keenan, an expert in Soviet behavior, is credited with initiating the United States' containment policy against communism that prevailed at the start of the Cold War.

of life in this region, also known as the Communist bloc. The Soviet government controlled all the media in the USSR and played a large role in controlling the media in the states of Eastern Europe. All news and current affairs programs were filtered through state censors and were filled with propaganda that played up the strengths of communism and the weaknesses of the West. What passed for fact was often fiction, and citizens could not be sure what was real information and what was merely propaganda. Individuals were not allowed to speak out against their government. Those brave enough to challenge the system found themselves without jobs, exiled, jailed, or even killed. Dissent was not tolerated.

America Develops a Strategy

By 1947 Communist movements of varying intensity were taking place all over Europe, and there was great debate in the United States over how to address the situation. A civil war in Greece was beginning to swing in the direction of the Communists, and the Soviets were trying to force Turkey to hand over control of the Dardanelles and the Bosporus Strait, which connected the Black Sea to the Mediterranean.

The United States was reluctant to engage in what it called "atomic diplomacy," threatening the use of atomic weapons to alter Soviet behavior. After the devastation that had been brought on Japan, the United States only wanted to use the atomic bomb as a weapon of last resort. Additionally, according to

Friedman, "through 1947, the U.S. nuclear threat was largely a bluff. The stockpile was so embarrassingly small that the number of bombs was not even committed to paper."[7]

Truman decided to use America's economic might as a weapon to fight communism. On March 12, 1947, he asked a joint session of Congress to approve $300 million for Greece and $100 million for Turkey to help them fight the Communist insurgencies in their countries. In what would become known as the Truman Doctrine, the president said, "It must be the policy of the United States to support free peoples who are resisting attempted subjugation by armed minorities or outside pressures."[8] The Truman Doctrine was the first step in the creation of a strategy for dealing with the spread of Soviet influence in Europe. It established America's position as a defender of free nations. The development of the policy of containment would lay a blueprint for how America would respond to Soviet aggression.

Containment policy was attributed to George Kennan, director of the Policy Planning Staff in the State Department, a new organization committed to creating new foreign policy ideas. Kennan wrote an article in 1947 titled "The Sources of Soviet Conduct" that detailed the reasoning behind Soviet policy, and it would become the basis for how to effectively counter Soviet actions. "It must be inevitably assumed in Moscow," wrote Kennan, "that the aims of the capitalist world are antagonistic to the Soviet regime. . . . From [its ideology] flow many of the phenomena which we find disturbing in the Kremlin's conduct of foreign policy: the secretiveness, the lack of frankness, the duplicity, the wary suspiciousness, and the basic unfriendliness of purpose."[9]

Containing the Communist threat within its preexisting borders required the United States to be open about its disagreements with the Soviets. The United States would no longer make any concessions to Soviet demands to expand its control beyond its present borders; however, the United States would not make any efforts to liberate areas already under Soviet control. America would also have to reconstitute its military, which had been significantly reduced from an active-duty military of 12 million in 1945 to 1.5 million just two years later. The Soviet armed forces, by comparison, numbered 4 million in 1947.

Truman was reluctant to increase military spending, but he did sign the National Security Act on July 26, 1947, to reorganize the Army, Navy, Marines, and Air Force as distinct branches under a Department of Defense. The cabinet-level post of secretary of war was changed to secretary of defense, with U.S. Navy secretary James Forrestal appointed as the first person to hold the post.

The National Security Act established the National Security Council (NSC), a group of presidential advisers who would meet regularly to make foreign policy recommendations based on intelligence collected by various agencies, including the Central Intelligence Agency (CIA), which was also created under the act. The CIA had certain essential duties that included the collection of intelligence, the production of intelligence estimates and reports for the NSC, and performing "such other functions and duties related to intelligence affecting the national security as the President of the National Security Council may direct."[10]

A larger military alone would not contain communism. According to Kennan, containment had to be a multi-layered strategy that relied on a complex combination of America's economic, political, and military strengths to provide a counterforce to meet the Soviets at every point where they threatened American allies and interests. He noted, "As things stand today, it is not Russian military power which is threatening us, it is Russian political power. . . . If it is not entirely a military threat, I doubt that it can be effectively met entirely by military means."[11]

The Marshall Plan

Russian political power was a serious threat in Europe due to the poor economic conditions across the continent. Postwar recovery was tediously slow, and the harsh winter of 1946–1947 caused many to lose hope. America's leaders recognized that if something drastic was not done soon, the bad economy would lead to political unrest and increased Soviet influence. The solution that was crafted was the European Recovery Program, popularly known as the Marshall Plan, after the program's principal author, Secretary of State George C. Marshall. The plan called for massive

A worker participates in the reconstruction of a concert hall in West Berlin in 1950 as part of the European Recovery Program. Also known as the Marshall Plan, the U.S.-backed program provided loans to help the countries devastated by World War II rebuild their infrastructure and economies.

loans to European nations based on their specific economic needs. American and European bankers determined these needs by closely examining the borrowers' budget documents. A strict provision of the loan was that the money had to be used to buy American products and services. This direct return on investment was the only way the U.S. government could guarantee that the Marshall fund would remain solvent.

Marshall said on June 5, 1947, "It is logical that the United States should do whatever it is able to do to assist the return of normal economic health in the world, without which there can be no political stability and no assured peace."[12] The program did not discriminate among nations based on the political leanings of their governments. Over the next year, twenty-two European nations were invited to join the recovery program, including the nations of the Communist bloc. The Soviets rejected the offer on behalf of its satellite states because they believed that entry into the program would lead to their becoming slaves to the American economy.

Truman signed the Marshall Plan into law on April 3, 1948. Over the next four years $13 billion worth of aid would flow to Europe. Within two years, overall industrial production rose 62 percent, and agricultural production rose by 10 percent. French industrial output was 50 percent higher than in 1939. Foreign trade doubled in the German sector under Allied control; however, more effort beyond Marshall Plan funding was needed to get Germany back on its feet. The United States shouldered much of the economic burden for the western half of Germany, and it wanted to bring its role to an end. As historian Martin Walker notes in *The Cold War: A History*, "For the American zone commander, General Lucius Clay, the solution was plain; the German economy had to be freed from the constraints of occupation."[13]

The U.S., French, and British governments introduced the German deutsche mark on June 18, 1948. The Soviets were angered by this move because they believed that the new currency would lead to U.S. dominance over Berlin. On June 24 the Soviets cut off all access to the city.

The Soviets Blockade Berlin

All rail, road, and water access to Berlin was cut off to the Allies, leaving the citizens of West Berlin at the mercy of the Soviets. Stalin hoped that the United States would give up and leave Berlin for good, but Truman knew that such a move would permanently harm American prestige. If the United States could not be counted on to defend West Berlin, then its resolve in other parts of Europe would also be questioned.

Rather than forcibly clear the road in the Soviet sector to reach West Berlin, U.S. Air Force generals Hap Arnold and Curtis LeMay suggested an airlift to bring supplies into the city. The Berlin Airlift, commonly known at the time as Operation Vittles, was born.

Over the course of the next eleven months, U.S. and British pilots conducted more than 278,000 flights that delivered 2.3 million tons of food, fuel, and such morale-building supplies as toys, clothes, and candy to the citizens of West Berlin. The pilots flew within three open-air corridors that were 20 miles (32km) wide and often risked midair collisions and crash landings on the short runways in the city.

The longer the airlift lasted, the more smoothly the operation went. Although the Soviets had hoped to squeeze the city into submission, West Berlin's citizens began to live more comfortably as the daily food ration rose from 1,600 to 1,880 calories per day. In fact, many Berliners actually started gaining weight during the blockade.

German children cheer as a U.S. cargo plane brings provisions to West Berlin in 1948 as part of Operation Vittles, a program to airlift food and supplies following the Soviet blockade that cut off the Allies' road, rail, and water access to the region.

On May 12, 1949, the Soviets recognized they had nothing to gain by maintaining their siege on the city, and the blockade came to an end. The Americans had proven their dedication to protecting their allies. The official creation of West Germany in September made it clear that the country would not be reunited anytime soon. Germany was now two distinct nations; one democratic and the other Communist.

The Creation of NATO

The blockade of Berlin and the fall of Czechoslovakia and Hungary to the Communists in 1948 and 1949 caused serious concern among Western European nations. The Soviets maintained a garrison of thirty divisions in Eastern and Central Europe, while the United States, France, and Great Britain fielded a total of ten divisions combined. A proposal was made among the Allies to forge an alliance to prevent the further spread of communism on the continent.

The North Atlantic Treaty, which was signed on April 4, 1949, caused concern among traditional American isolationists, who were against entering into military alliances with other nations. This sentiment was overcome by recognizing that America was the only country in the world that could protect free nations from the giant Soviet military machine.

Radio Free Europe

Radio Free Europe (RFE) went on the air in 1950 to offer an alternative news source to people living inside the Communist bloc. RFE was a private, nonprofit corporation that was supervised by a board appointed by the U.S. president and funded by the Central Intelligence Agency until 1971 and by the U.S. Congress thereafter. RFE operated from transmitters located in Munich, West Germany, and sent its signals into Poland, Hungary, Czechoslovakia, Bulgaria, and Romania. Radio Liberty (RL), an offspring of RFE created in 1953, focused its broadcasts specifically on Russia.

The Soviets worked ceaselessly to prevent the broadcasts. Cissie Dore Hill, curator of the RFE records archive at the Hoover Institution, a pubic-policy research center, explains:

The communist governments responded to the unwelcome radios by jamming their signals—broadcasting shrieks, howls, white noise, or other electronic sounds on the same frequencies—so that it was difficult or impossible to hear the program from RFE or RL. Jamming was done by the Soviet Union continually from within the first 10 minutes of programming in 1953 through most of 1988. The five RFE target countries all jammed at various times during the Cold War. In addition, the communist governments, viewing the émigré employees as traitors to their homelands, threatened employees and their families still living behind the Iron Curtain and carried out assassinations and bombings. Spies infiltrated the radios, some occupying key positions.

Despite the efforts of the Communists, RFE and RL continued to broadcast throughout the Cold War and continue to operate today in twenty-eight languages throughout Europe and Asia.

Cissie Dore Hill, "Voices of Hope: The Story of Radio Free Europe and Radio Liberty," *Hoover Digest*, no. 4, 2001. www.hoover.org/publications/digest/3475896.html.

The original members of the North Atlantic Treaty Organization (NATO) were the United States, Great Britain, Canada, Iceland, France, Belgium, the Netherlands, Luxembourg, Norway, Denmark, Portugal, and Italy. NATO was meant to be more than just a military alliance, but its principal provision was Article 5, which basically stated that an attack on any one member would be considered an attack on all members. The European members of NATO nearly doubled their defense spending to $8 billion in 1951.

In 1955 the Communist bloc responded with a similar treaty organization, known as the Warsaw Pact.

Operating under a defense provision identical to NATO's Article 5, the Communist nations of Albania, Bulgaria, East Germany, Hungary, Poland, Romania, and the USSR agreed to mutually defend one another from an attack by any opposing force.

The USSR Becomes a Nuclear Power

America's monopoly over nuclear weapons ended on August 29, 1949, when the Soviets successfully tested an atomic bomb in Kazakhstan. The weapon had a yield of 22 kilotons and was of the same design as the U.S. atomic bombs that were developed in 1945. The United States became aware of the test after routine surveillance flights near the Soviet borders detected unusually high amounts of radiation in the atmosphere.

America was shocked at this development because intelligence estimates predicted the Soviets were two or three years away from developing an atomic weapon. It was discovered that Klaus Fuchs, a German émigré who was among the team of scientists who developed America's atomic bomb, had passed secrets to the Soviets during the final months of World War II

What Is a *Cold War*?

A cold war is a conflict that is engaged in by two opposing forces via means other than direct military confrontation, or a hot war. Politician and financier Bernard Baruch first applied the term cold war to the conflict between the United States and the Soviet Union. During a speech he gave on April 16, 1947, Baruch stated:

Let us not be deceived—we are today in the midst of a cold war. Our enemies are to be found abroad and at home. Let us never forget this: Our unrest is the heart of their success. The peace of the world is the hope and the goal of our political system; it is the despair and defeat of those who stand against us. We can depend only on ourselves.

The United States and the Soviet Union competed on many fronts during nearly five decades of conflict, including the fields of politics, diplomacy, commerce, industry, technology, and even sports. Both countries sent many men to war during that time, but in all the wars that were fought between the forces of democracy and the forces of communism, Americans and Russians never once met on the field of battle.

Quoted in History.com, "Bernard Baruch Coins the Term 'Cold War,'" April 16, 1947. www.history.com/this-day-in-history.do?action=tdihArticleCategory&displayDate=04/16&categoryId=coldwar.

because he believed that Russia needed to know what its allies had accomplished.

News of the Soviet test, which Americans referred to as Joe 1 after Joseph Stalin, forced the United States to reevaluate its strategic posture. Truman ordered a full analysis of America's national security policy. It was deter-mined, states historian Friedman, that "soon it would be impossible to use nuclear weapons to deal cheaply with a Soviet conventional attack. The Soviets might hit back with their own nuclear weapons. . . . Without superior overall military power, containment would be no more than a bluff."[14]

Chapter Two

New Commitments, New Dangers

"We had hoped that the Soviet Union, with its security assured by the Charter of the United Nations, would be willing to live and let live. But I am sorry to say that has not been the case."
—President Harry S. Truman,
State of the Union Address,
January 8, 1951

The depth of America's commitment to protect the free nations of Europe did not stop the Soviets from attempting to realize their dream of a worldwide Communist revolution. Their willingness to subvert democracy and overthrow sovereign governments proved their own commitment to their cause, and their acquisition of the atomic bomb in 1949 raised the stakes of the contest. Now both nations had the power to level entire cities with the use of a single weapon. This was an unsettling thought to American military planners, who were already aware of the distinct advantage the USSR held in conventional armed forces.

As the military situation became more complex and more dangerous, the front on which the Cold War was fought began to shift. By 1949 the lines in Europe had stabilized, with the Soviets having pushed as far west as they could without risking war with America, but dramatic changes were taking place in Asia. America's postwar occupation of Japan was turning the former imperial power into a democratic nation with a strong economy, but it was a lone point of stability in the region. A civil war in China between Communists and Nationalists had been raging since 1927. Anticolonial movements in Korea, French Indochina, and elsewhere also gave rise to Communist insurgencies.

China Falls to the Communists

Since 1927 the Communist forces of Mao Zedong had been fighting with the Nationalist government, run by Chiang Kai-shek, to gain control of China. Over the

Communist forces fly banners depicting their leaders in June 1949 in Shanghai, China, following that city's fall to the People's Liberation Army during the Chinese Civil War.

next twenty years, through the Japanese occupation and withdrawal, the Communists solidified their power in northern China. Stalin aided Mao and the Nationalists because he preferred a divided nation on Russia's eastern border. He recognized that Mao was a committed Communist with an independent mind and that he would not willingly take orders from Moscow.

By 1948 the grip that Chiang's Nationalists held over the country began to slip. The government was weak and corrupt and the economy suffered severe inflation, leading many to doubt Chiang's ability to lead. The army, which had suffered the loss of tens of thousands of officers during World War II, was poorly led. Only 27 percent of the division commanders had any formal military training. Many of the troops were reluctant to fight, and they were poor fighters when they could be convinced to engage the Communists. Many more refused to fight at night because they did not know the terrain and the Communists had grown skilled at nighttime raids.

Chiang turned to the United States for help, but Truman made up his mind as far back as 1946 that saving China was not worth the price the United States would have to pay. As historian Martin Walker writes, $2 billion in aid had already been given to no avail. America, Walker explains, "would virtually have to take over the Chinese government. . . . It would involve the U.S. in a continuing commitment from which it would be practically impossible to withdraw."[15] Chiang's forces fled to the island of Formosa in the South China Sea, and on October 1, 1949, Mao declared victory. The world's most populous nation had become Communist.

Who Lost China?

Even before China fell to Mao's forces, President Truman was the target of mounting criticism over his stance on communism. He received some level of blame for each Eastern European country that slipped behind the Iron Curtain. In the presidential election of 1948, Truman, a Democrat, faced harsh accusations from Republicans that he was not up to the fight against the Soviet Union. His most extreme critics believed any move short of forcibly ejecting the Soviets from Eastern Europe amounted to appeasement. Truman won reelection by a narrow margin, but his political fortunes did not improve.

The loss of China to the Communists and Truman's refusal to provide additional aid to Chiang Kai-shek on Formosa led to the charge that he was soft on communism. During the Cold War, being labeled as such was considered the worst political attack that could be suffered by a president. The CIA and the Joint Chiefs of Staff agreed that Formosa, later known as Taiwan, was of little strategic value. Secretary of State Dean Acheson argued that Chiang's fall was not due to a lack of American support. "Chiang Kai-shek had emerged from [World War II] as the leader of the Chinese people, opposed by only one faction, the ragged, ill-equipped, small Communist force in the hills," Acheson noted. "Four years later his armies and his support both within the country and outside it had melted away."[16]

Republicans in Congress rejected this view, choosing to believe that statements about Chiang's ineffective leadership were excuses to cover up a "wishful, do-nothing policy which has succeeded only in placing Asia in danger of Soviet conquest, with its ultimate threat to the peace of the world and our own national security."[17]

The debate over just who was responsible for China succumbing to communism never reached a satisfactory conclusion. The domestic political struggle had to take a backseat to the troubling reality that with China and the Soviet Union as allies, much of the Eurasian landmass was under Communist control. Republicans and Democrats alike recognized that communism in Asia would not stop at China's border.

A Proposed Shift in American Strategy

American policy planners had to rethink the country's containment strategy as the battle to contain communism expanded to new regions. Containment, as George Kennan had defined it, was based on keeping the Soviets from threatening American allies and interests. Paul Nitze, who replaced Kennan as the director of Policy Planning for the State Department in 1949, viewed containment as a more comprehensive strategy that basically called for a perimeter defense that would encircle the Communist bloc of Eastern Europe and Asia to prevent it from stretching any farther.

Nitze and several members of the State and Defense departments wrote a secret memorandum for Truman that included this new vision of containment and how it could be achieved. The memo, commonly known as National Security Council Memorandum 68, or simply NSC-68, outlined an aggressive strategy that called for the United States to undergo significant military rearmament in order to meet Soviet force with equal or greater force anywhere in the world.

Truman was initially resistant to NSC-68 in part due to the cost. The conversion from the high wartime production of World War II to a slower manufacturing peacetime pace had already caused a slowdown in the economy. Truman did not want to further stress it with the high taxes and budget deficits that would come with a military buildup. Another concern for the president was that a conventional arms buildup would lead to an arms race with the Soviets.

Nitze argued that the Soviet arms industry was already operating at full capacity, devoting 40 percent of Soviet resources to military production. Additionally, estimates of the Soviets' nuclear potential suggested that, by 1954, the Soviets would be capable of seriously damaging the United States in a coordinated atomic attack.

Truman remained unconvinced that the policy shift outlined in NSC-68 was the way to go. His advisers cautioned against supporting it openly because they did not believe Congress would authorize the increase in military spending that the strategy outlined as necessary to combat the Soviets.

The Korean War

While American politicians debated how best to combat the spread of communism in the spring of 1950, CIA analysts were observing an unprecedented troop buildup in North Korea, a Communist nation in Asia supported by Stalin. Despite the recent events in China, civilian leaders in Washington did not believe this would lead to invasion of democratic South Korea. On June 20 Dean Rusk, the assistant secretary of state for Far Eastern affairs, told Congress that he saw no evidence of war brewing on the Korean peninsula.

America had maintained a troop presence in Korea since the region was freed from the Japanese at the end of World War II. The peninsula was divided along the 38th parallel between the Soviet Union, which occupied the northern half of the country, and the United States, which controlled the southern half. The Soviets set up a Communist government in their sector, while the United States formed a democratic nation in the south. In 1948 the United Nations moved to hold elections that would unify the country, but the North Koreans refused to participate because they feared losing the election to the larger population of South Korea.

North Korean leader Kim Il Sung wanted Stalin to support a forced reunification of the country under the Communist banner. Stalin was initially reluctant to take on the United States. By 1950, however, he thought a united Korea would be a good counterbalance to Japan, which was rebuilding rapidly as an economic power under U.S. protection.

Ten divisions of the North Korean army, equipped with the latest Soviet weapons and artillery, marched south across the 38th parallel in the early morning hours of June 25, 1950. The large invasion force moved swiftly, wiping out the token resistance put up by South Korean and American troops caught completely by surprise.

American politicians in Washington were also caught unaware. Truman convened a war council on June 27 to discuss options. Rusk told the president, "A South Korea absorbed by the communists would be a dagger pointed at the heart of Japan."[18]

The United Nations condemned the North Korean action and pledged support to South Korea. The United States would provide the bulk of the troops and matériel for the UN force, but fifteen other nations would also provide manpower and logistical support. The Soviet Union remained silent during the UN vote because it had earlier boycotted the

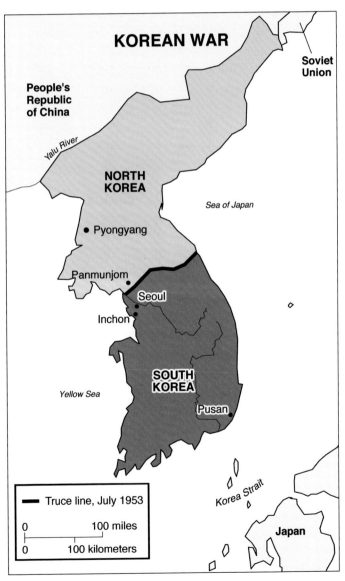

The Korean peninsula remained divided into two countries demarked by a truce line after three years of war between the Chinese-backed Communists of North Korea and the United Nations-supported South Korean forces led by the United States.

General Douglas MacArthur, seated, arrives in September 1950 at South Korea's Inchon Harbor. It was here where UN forces under his command landed behind enemy lines to drive back a North Korean advance into the southern tip of the Korean peninsula.

organization for not allowing Communist China to become a permanent member of the UN Security Council along with itself, the United States, France, and Great Britain.

UN support could not come fast enough. U.S. and South Korean troops were quickly driven to the southern tip of the Korean peninsula before the advancing North Korean army. On September 15 U.S. forces under the command of General Douglas MacArthur made an amphibious landing behind enemy lines at Inchon. The North Korean advance rapidly disintegrated and was driven back across the 38th parallel with South Korea and its allied forces in pursuit.

A debate over how to handle the Ko-

rean conflict arose, however, as MacArthur made his way into North Korea. The general had a reputation as a brilliant strategist and was a genuine hero of World War II, but where Truman wanted only to protect South Korea, MacArthur saw in his command a mandate to "to clear out all of Korea, to unify it, and to liberalize it."[19]

Truman was concerned that the conflict could start a third world war. China might enter the war on behalf of North Korea if it felt threatened by MacArthur's advance. The Soviets could take advantage of the situation by making a move against Western Europe, recognizing that America did not have the military might to defend Korea and Europe simultaneously. This was also the first conflict in which both sides had access to atomic weapons, a fact that played a role in every decision the president made.

MacArthur assured Truman that the Chinese would not get involved and suggested publicly that if they did, dropping atomic bombs on the Chinese mainland would quickly bring an end to their role

Matthew Ridgway: The Man Who Saved Korea

Much has been written about how General Douglas MacArthur's landing at Inchon turned the tide of the Korean War in 1950, routing North Korean forces from the south. However, when the Chinese army swarmed into North Korea and pushed the American forces back south later that year, the task of leading the demoralized Eighth U.S. Army fell to General Matthew Ridgway, one of the most capable but least known commanders in American military history. Historian Thomas Fleming writes:

In his first forty-eight hours, Ridgway had met with all his American corps and division commanders and all but one of the Republic of Korea division commanders. He told them . . . that he had no plans whatsoever to evacuate Korea. . . . He cabled the Pentagon that he wanted to relieve almost every division commander and artillery commander. . . . The ineffective generals were sent home singly over the next few months. . . .

Regimental, division, and corps commanders were told . . . that it was time to abandon creature comforts and shed their timidity about getting off the roads and into the hills, where the enemy was holding the high ground. Again and again Ridgway repeated the ancient army slogan "Find them! Fix them! Fight them! Finish them!"

Thomas Fleming, *The Cold War: A Military History.* New York: Random House, 2005, p. 112.

Under the command of General Matthew Ridgway, the demoralized UN forces shored up their efforts to push back their Communist opponents during the Korean War.

in the conflict. The general's assurances and threats did not have any effect on the Chinese, who, on October 19, sent 150,000 soldiers across the border to support the weary North Korean armed forces. Together they drove U.S. forces south again.

MacArthur's failure to properly assess the Chinese response did not sit well with Truman. The general's increasingly bold public pronouncements that blamed Truman for the present situation in Korea also demonstrated disrespect for the constitutional mandate that the president was the commander in chief of the armed forces. On April 11 Truman issued a statement that said, "I have concluded that General of the Army Douglas MacArthur is unable to give his wholehearted support to the policies of the United States Government and of the United Nations. . . . I have, therefore, relieved General MacArthur of his commands."[20]

The war in Korea went on for two more years with neither side gaining any significant ground. After July 1951 the front lines did not shift far from the point where the war had started in June 1950. By the time the armistice to cease hostilities was signed on July 27, 1953, 35,000 American soldiers had died in the war. Total casualties for North and South Koreans and Chinese are widely disputed, but close to 2 million Korean soldiers and civilians lost their lives in a war in which no territory or political power changed hands.

In contrast, much had changed in America. Martin Walker notes, "American diplomacy, defense budgets and military reach exploded across the globe in the aftermath of the invasion, as U.S. taxpayers and Congress alike gave the unstinted support the strategic planners had [previously] sought with only limited success."[21] In Washington the debate over the policy of NSC-68 came to an end, and Congress approved a dramatic increase in defense spending. The defense budget rose from $13.7 billion in 1950 to $24 billion in 1951. It would rise again in 1952 to $46 billion.

The Cold War Comes Home

The American public had watched with fear and uncertainty as the events in Korea unfolded half a world away. The price of stopping communism had been rising steadily since the late 1940s, yet the USSR seemed bent on continuing its march toward world domination. The Soviets' possession of the atomic bomb unnerved U.S. citizens even more because they believed that the Communists were willing to use it without provocation. The popular U.S. view was that the Communists did not place a high value on life like Americans. Massive casualties in a U.S. counterattack would not deter the Soviets if they believed they could achieve any advantage.

This bleak view of the Soviets developed through a combination of factors. communism was completely opposed to the American democratic ideal and openly called for the defeat of free-market capitalism. The secretive and brutal nature of the Soviet government and its expansionist foreign policy directly threatened America's allies. Perhaps the most significant factor was the discovery

Alger Hiss, a State Department official accused of being a Communist, takes the stand under oath before giving his testimony to the House Un-American Activities Committee in August 1948.

of Communist sympathizers and spies in the United States.

The atomic spy ring that aided the Soviets in developing their atomic bomb in 1949 was the first major indication that America was at risk within its own borders. Scientist Klaus Fuchs was only one of a number of people who were arrested and charged with espionage. Lisle A. Rose details the extent of the plot in *The Cold War Comes to Main Street: America in 1950*: "Fuchs had given his information to . . . Harry Gold. Gold, in turn, had been part of a wartime Soviet spy ring that included U.S. Army Corporal David Greenglass . . . and Ethel and Julius Rosenberg, who had funneled the information they received from Gold and Greenglass directly to their Soviet contacts."[22]

Fuchs, Greenglass, and Gold were all sentenced to lengthy prison terms, but the Rosenbergs' direct contact with Soviet agents and their complete refusal to cooperate with authorities led to death sentences for both the husband and wife. They were executed on June 19, 1953.

The atomic spy ring motivated Congress to increase its efforts to root out Communist sympathizers both in the government and in private society. The House Un-American Activities Committee (HUAC), created in 1938 to locate Nazi sympathizers in the government, shifted its focus to communism. Truman believed that HUAC wasted its time in investigating the government, but the August 3, 1948, testimony of *Time* magazine editor Whitaker Chambers led many elected officials to a different conclusion.

Chambers, an admitted former Communist, accused State Department diplomat Alger Hiss of being a Communist with whom he had associated during the 1930s. This charge created a great stir in the media. Hiss was well respected among Democrats in the diplomatic community, with Truman, Acheson, and Illinois governor Adlai Stevenson among his top supporters. He was one of the top Americans involved in the formation of the United Nations, and even the Soviet Union petitioned for him to be the organization's first secretary-general.

New Commitments, New Dangers ■ 33

Dean Acheson's Speech at Berkeley

Dean Acheson served as one of Harry Truman's top advisers, playing a key role in the formation of the Truman Doctrine, the Marshall Plan, and NATO. By the time Acheson became secretary of state in 1949, communism seemed on an unstoppable roll across Europe and Asia. Truman and Acheson were both criticized in America for not being tough enough with the Soviets.

On March 16, 1950, Acheson gave a speech in Berkeley, California, that proved to his critics that he was anything but soft on communism. Historian Robert L. Beisner writes:

[A cheson] left the strong implication that the Soviets had first to prove their wish for peace. . . . In short, these were preconditions for talks: (1) German unification . . . under a freely elected government; (2) withdrawal of Soviet troops from Austria; (3) an end to obstructionism against a Japanese peace treaty; (4) peaceful unification of Korea through free elections; (5) withdrawal of Soviet troops and police from the eastern European "satellite area"; (6) an end to "obstruction" in the UN; (7) cooperation in making "realistic" progress in arms control (including nuclear weapons); (8) an end to subverting other governments . . . ; (9) decent and respectful treatment of foreign diplomats in Moscow; and (10) a halt to hostile and violent Soviet propaganda.

Acheson did not believe that the Soviets would meet all or even some of the conditions he outlined, but at least America's views were out in the open.

Robert L. Beisner, *Dean Acheson: A Life in the Cold War.* New York: Oxford University Press, 2006, p. 249.

Hiss flatly denied the charges, but Chambers had the strong support of Republican congressman Richard Nixon of California. When Hiss testified before HUAC to clear his name, Nixon grew suspicious of his contradictory answers to questions about his alleged involvement with the Communist Party and his association with Chambers. Hiss was later convicted of two counts of perjury for lying under oath and was sent to prison. Nixon's pursuit of Hiss made him an anti-Communist hero and directly led to his election to the U.S. Senate in 1950.

The Red Scare

Republican senator Joseph McCarthy of Wisconsin also made a name for himself as a staunch anti-Communist, and his zealous pursuit of Soviet agents in America created an era of mistrust in America. McCarthy boldly claimed at a rally in 1950, "I have in my hand 57 cases of individuals who would appear to be either card-carrying members or certainly loyal to the Communist Party."[23]

McCarthy frequently changed the number of people he claimed to know were Communists in the State Department or the Truman administration, and he never backed up his allegations with hard evidence, but it did not matter. He believed that Communists—or "commies," "reds," or "pinkos," as they were frequently referred to in the United States—had infiltrated numerous areas of American life and had to be rooted out by any means necessary.

The few legitimate cases of Communist subversion, like Hiss and the Rosenbergs, had led politicians and the public to fear that Communists were everywhere. Mistrust of people who were law-abiding American citizens was common. Everyone who worked in the State Department was required to take a loyalty oath to prove that he or she was an American patriot. This practice went on in numerous other professions, including the motion-picture industry, where Screen Actors Guild president Ronald Reagan installed a loyalty oath as a prerequisite for joining the union.

As McCarthy grew more powerful, his charges grew wilder, yet no one wanted to challenge him for fear of facing accusations of being a Communist. In the spring of 1954, McCarthy baselessly claimed that the U.S. Army was plagued by Communist infiltration. The televised Senate hearings that followed this charge pitted McCarthy against Army counsel Joseph Welch who, unmoved by McCarthy's tirades, asked the senator, "At long last, have you no sense of decency, sir?"[24]

The Army-McCarthy hearings marked the end of the senator's reckless pursuit of Communists. On December 2, 1954, the Senate voted 67–22 to censure McCarthy for "contemptuous conduct." He quietly served out the remainder of his term and

Republican senator Joseph McCarthy, who led an impassioned and often reckless crusade against Communist influences in the United States, testifies about alleged Communist Party activity across the country during the Army-McCarthy hearings in June 1954.

Blacklisting and the Hollywood Ten

In its fervor to uncover Communist subversion in Cold War America, the House Un-American Activities Committee (HUAC) focused much of its energies on the entertainment industry. It was believed that Communist infiltration in motion pictures could greatly influence public opinion because of America's love of the movies. During the height of the HUAC investigations, from 1947 to 1951, many of Hollywood's top producers, directors, and stars were called before the committee. Authors Jeremy Isaacs and Taylor Downing write:

Elia Kazan, the Academy Award–winning director who first put Marlon Brando on the screen, named eleven former Communists before the HUAC. Jerome Robbins, the successful Broadway and Hollywood choreographer, agreed to cooperate with the committee. [Actor] Sterling Hayden did the same. Screenwriter Martin Berkeley broke the record by naming 162 Hollywood artists as former or present-day Communists. Some 250 Hollywood personalities were blacklisted [banned from working in Hollywood]. . . . They included some of the most talented directors, writers, and performers in the industry.

Nine screenwriters and one director who refused to comply with the HUAC's questioning (and were, in fact, previously or currently members of the Communist Party) went to jail for contempt of Congress. They were Alvah Bessie, Herbert Biberman, Lester Cole, Edward Dmytryk, Ring Lardner Jr., John Howard Lawson, Albert Maltz, Samuel Ornitz, Adrian Scott, and Dalton Trumbo. This Hollywood Ten, as they came to be known, were officially banned from working in Hollywood for many years, but some continued to work under pseudonyms. Trumbo even received an Academy Award for best screenplay in 1956.

Jeremy Isaacs and Taylor Downing, *Cold War: An Illustrated History, 1945–1991.* New York: Little, Brown, 1998, p.113.

died on May 2, 1957, at the age of forty-eight of health complications brought on by years of rampant alcoholism.

The extreme paranoia that McCarthy created pitted Americans against each other. The real, though overblown, threat of Communist subversion in the American government did not justify the mis-trust of friends, family, and coworkers that marked the period known as the Red Scare. However, domestic fears of the Soviet Union and its expansionist policies did not die with McCarthy. A new era of missile technology and more powerful weapons made the threat graver and more real than ever.

Chapter Three

The Cold War Goes Global

"*I know not with what weapons World War III will be fought, but World War IV will be fought with sticks and stones.*"

—Albert Einstein, in a letter to President Harry S. Truman

General Dwight David "Ike" Eisenhower was elected president of the United States in 1952 on the Republican ticket over Democrat Adlai Stevenson. His impeccable military credentials as the liberator of Europe during World War II and the staunch anti-communism of his vice president, Richard Nixon, assured Americans that the country would be ably led in an age of tense conflict with the Soviet Union. Eisenhower noted in his inaugural address on January 20, 1953, "Conceiving the defense of freedom, like freedom itself, to be one and indivisible, we hold all continents and peoples in equal regard and honor."[25] It was clear that the new president intended to continue the policy of meeting and preventing the expansion of communism on every front.

The Soviet Union also experienced a change in leadership. Joseph Stalin, leader of the USSR for twenty-nine years, died on March 15, 1953, after suffering a stroke. Stalin's iron rule resulted in numerous crimes against his people, yet many Russians admired him for transforming the Soviet Union from a poor agricultural nation to a world power. There was a bitter contest to succeed him, and eventually Nikita Khrushchev emerged to become the leader of the USSR.

Khrushchev was not ruthless like Stalin, but this did not mean by any sense that the Cold War was over. Khrushchev was a true Communist committed to worldwide revolution, and the Soviet quest for greater power continued under his leadership.

The New Look and Massive Retaliation

The bleak worldview held by the American foreign policy establishment at the beginning of the Eisenhower administration was best illustrated by his secretary of state, John Foster Dulles, "Already one-third of the world is dominated by an imperialistic brand of communism; already the free world has been so shrunk that no further substantial points of it can be lost without danger to the whole that remains."[26]

Previous attempts to stem the tide of communism had met with mixed results. Containment, as George Kennan had envisioned it, stabilized Europe but could not prevent the fall of China or Communist uprisings throughout Asia. NSC-68 had come too late to prevent the Korean War, and the American public did not want to be continuously sending its sons off to fight wars in foreign lands.

Eisenhower had every intention of protecting the free world from Communist aggression as Truman had before him, but the United States could not hope to engage the Soviets on every front with an equal show of force, as NSC-68 had called for and as Eisenhower himself had promised in his inaugural address. The cost of building and maintaining the conventional armed forces needed for such an undertaking was staggering even for America's robust economy. In Eisenhower's view, Amer-

President Dwight Eisenhower (left) and Secretary of State John Foster Dulles (right) advocated a defensive stance called the New Look, which called for the United States to assemble a huge arsenal of nuclear weapons that the country would be prepared to use in response to a Soviet military threat.

ica could not be turned into a military state through massive defense spending or the very concept of freedom that America stood for would be lost.

Eisenhower decided to combat the cost problem by relying on a strategic framework called the New Look. The New Look essentially put the majority of America's defense resources into building a nuclear arsenal of such magnitude that the Soviets would never dare militarily challenge the United States.

The New Look defense posture was key to the broader policy of massive retaliation. Dulles defined this new doctrine by stating that "the way to deter aggression is for the free community to be willing and able to respond vigorously at places and with means of its own choosing."[27] Under this strategy, the United States was prepared to use whatever response it deemed necessary to counter a Soviet threat against America or its allies.

Critics like Adlai Stevenson, Senator John F. Kennedy, and Harvard political scholar Henry Kissinger disputed the wisdom of this policy because it did not give the United States any flexibility to deal diplomatically with the Soviets. It seemed hard to imagine that the United States would risk the destruction of its own cities in a nuclear war over a border dispute in some third-world country.

Dulles argued that massive retaliation actually provided the United States with more flexibility, not less. Rather than trying to match the Soviets soldier for soldier or tank for tank, the United States would use its strengths—air and naval power and nuclear weapons—to keep Communist aggression in check. According to Dulles, America could then respond "effectively on a selective basis. . . . The method of do-ing so will vary according to the character of the various areas."[28]

Nuclear Testing

America's greater reliance on nuclear weapons meant that more weapons had to be tested to verify their effectiveness. The United States officially conducted 1,054 test detonations between 1945 and 1992, but the tests conducted during the 1950s were of special interest because of their scientific and military value. The scores of tests conducted in the atmosphere, underground, and underwater yielded new information on trigger mechanisms, detonation methods, and blast and radiation effects. Each new blast also served to remind Americans of the danger that existed from the Soviet possession of these terrifying weapons.

The first post–World War II tests of nuclear weapons took place in 1946 in the Marshall Islands in the western Pacific Ocean. Known as Operation Crossroads, nuclear bombs similar to the type used on Japan were detonated near decommissioned U.S. battleships to test the effects of the weapons on naval vessels. In some of the tests, live animals were placed on the ships to test the effects of heat and radiation from the blast.

Nuclear devices were tested in a variety of scenarios and locations. The South Pacific and the desert regions of Nevada and New Mexico were the most frequently used locations. Bombs were dropped from planes, were placed on 200-foot-tall (61m) towers and remotely detonated, and were detonated underground. Mock towns were built, complete with paved streets, automobiles, and homes filled with mannequins, to test blast effects on civilian structures. Troops conducted maneuvers just 6 miles (10km) from ground zero during the Buster-Jangle test of 1951.

The United States became interested in developing more powerful weapons as the Soviet nuclear arsenal grew in size. Scientist Edward Teller and mathematician Stanislaw Ulam believed that a more powerful weapon could be built using a fusion nuclear reaction rather than the fission reactions that powered the bombs previously built.

The first such bomb, a hydrogen bomb, was detonated on the island of Elugelab in the Marshall Islands on November 11, 1952. Codenamed "Mike," the bomb delivered an explosive power of ten megatons (equivalent to ten million tons of TNT) and completely vaporized the island. For miles in every direction, birds were burned out of the sky and fish were incinerated in the ocean. The fireball rose 57,000 feet (17,374m) into the air, and the mushroom cloud stretched 100 miles (161km). Scientist George Cowan, a witness to the blast, recalled, "As soon as I

A mushroom cloud rises above the Marshall Islands in November 1952 after the United States tested the detonation of the first hydrogen bomb. The cloud eventually extended 100 miles wide and reached 25 miles into the sky.

dared, I whipped off my dark glasses and the thing was enormous. . . . It looked as though it blotted out the whole horizon."[29]

An even more devastating test was conducted on March 1, 1954. Test detonation Bravo yielded fifteen megatons and resulted in the radiation exposure of 236 inhabitants of the Marshall Islands and the crew of a Japanese fishing boat that was in the vicinity of the blast. Elevated radiation levels from this test were detected around the globe.

Citizens all over the world expressed concern over the radioactive fallout that drifted into the atmosphere from the nuclear tests. The United States announced a suspension of nuclear testing on October 31, 1958, that lasted three years. The Soviets also suspended testing. This was the first instance that both countries engaged in any type of arms control, although the move was achieved without mutual agreement, and neither party was bound by treaty.

From Buildup to Mutual Assured Destruction

Larger and more destructive nuclear bombs were not the only strategic developments taking place during Eisenhower's presidency. America's total number of nuclear weapons increased dramatically. In 1949 there were 169 bombs in the U.S. arsenal; in 1957, there were 12,305. The methods of delivery also expanded. By 1960 significant strides in missile technology led to intercontinental ballistic missiles that could be fired from the United States and Europe to reach targets anywhere in the world.

Submarine-launched ballistic missiles were also introduced. There were more than fifteen hundred bomber planes stationed at bases around the world, including the B-52 long-range jet bomber, which was superior to any plane the Soviets possessed.

U.S. Air Force commanders were concerned that the Soviets were able to keep pace with America's strategic developments, and they warned Eisenhower of a potential missile gap in which the Soviets would possess more nuclear weapons than the United States. Eisenhower was not as concerned as the air force over the USSR's bomber developments, and he knew from American intelligence estimates that if any gap existed, it was in America's favor. The United States had 3,261 nuclear targets in the Soviet Union and the ability to hit nearly all of them four times. The Soviets did not have nearly as many nuclear weapons in their arsenal.

America's nuclear superiority did not provide any comfort to Eisenhower. Historian John Lewis Gaddis writes in *We Now Know: Rethinking Cold War History*, "Military superiority, [Eisenhower] understood better than anyone, guaranteed neither national nor international security. . . . If even a few [nuclear bombs] got through the effects would be as if thousands had."[30] The best that America could hope for was that the threat of massive retaliation would prevent nuclear war.

Fear of nuclear reprisal led to the idea of mutual assured destruction. Aptly known by its initials as MAD, this was a doctrine that came about by accident but was regarded as a credible deterrent. By the mid-1950s both the United States and the USSR had enough nuclear weapons to inflict crippling damage to each other. It was believed that neither country would risk a preemptive nuclear attack because any retaliatory strike would destroy them as well.

Both countries continued to build nuclear weapons long after they had achieved the ability to destroy their opponents because they sought a superior first-strike capability. If all the enemy's targets were wiped out in a first strike, then there would be no retaliation. Patrick Glynn, a former member of the U.S. Arms Control and Disarmament Agency, writes "The key to deterrence lay not in the overall size of the force but in the size of the force that could survive an enemy first strike."[31]

The Age of Intervention Begins

Neither America's nuclear supremacy nor threats of massive retaliation prevented the Soviet Union from seeking to expand its influence in the developing world. Khrushchev supported wars of liberation wherever Communist rebels were willing to accept Soviet aid. He sent military advisers, spies, money, and weapons around the world, all the while remaining below the combat threshold that could trigger the widespread U.S. response threatened by Dulles.

The postcolonial era that emerged after World War II created new opportunities for both the United States and the Soviet Union as they sought to enlist more allies to their respective causes. Between 1946 and 1960, thirty-seven new nations were created from the territories of shattered empires, and each one was a potential battleground in the worldwide struggle between democracy and communism. Eisenhower proclaimed, "As there is no weapon too small, no arena too remote, to be ignored, there is no free nation too humble to be forgotten."[32]

In Africa, Asia, Latin America, and the Middle East, conflict raged between local groups backed up by America and Russia. The Soviets supported Communist insurgents in their attempts to overthrow democratic or dictatorial regimes. They exploited economic and political discontent that was often found in emerging postcolonial nations. The United States, which prodded its allies France and Britain to relinquish their claims to empire after World War II, often found itself on the side of the dictators trying to defeat Communist movements or overthrow popular Communist regimes. As a result, America's well-intentioned defense against communism was often seen in the third world as support of imperialism and dictatorship.

America's involvement in the overthrow of the government of Mohammad Mossadegh in Iran in 1953 was the first of a string of interventions motivated by the U.S. promise to prevent the spread of communism. Mossadegh had nationalized assets of the Anglo-Iranian Oil Company, which is a process by which a government seizes the property of a privately held foreign company within its borders and takes control of that company. Mossadegh also accepted financial aid from the Soviets, prompting the CIA to stir up a coup that removed him from power in August. Hundreds were killed during the unrest that led to the installation of Shah Mohammad Reza Pahlavi as the pro-American leader of Iran. CIA operative Kermit Roosevelt noted afterward, "If we, the CIA are ever going to try something like this again, we must be absolutely sure that the people and the army want what we want. If not, you had better give the job to the Marines."[33]

Jacobo Arbenz Guzmán, the popularly elected leader of Guatemala, had nationalized assets of the United Fruit Company in 1954 and was receiving military aid from the USSR. The United States was not comfortable with an overt Communist influence in Central America and

Curtis "Bombs Away" LeMay

U.S. Air Force general Curtis LeMay was one of the most feared military minds of the Cold War, and that fear came mostly from American civilian leaders. LeMay, an outspoken tactician whose brutal air campaigns against Japanese targets helped bring World War II to a close, firmly believed in projecting an aggressive stance against the Soviets. LeMay led the Strategic Air Command (SAC), the U.S. Air Force nuclear bomber wing, from 1948 to 1957, and he later became the U.S. Air Force chief of staff.

As historian Victor Davis Hanson writes, LeMay may have been the symbol of military excess during the Cold War, but he possessed a unique understanding of the era.

[L eMay] was almost too quotable. The man who turned the Strategic Air Command into a justifiably feared instrument once said, "There are only two things in the world, SAC bases and SAC targets." Another time he said that the only foolproof antisubmarine system was "to boil the ocean with nukes." As for Cuba: "Fry it." Or North Vietnam: Bomb it "back into the Stone Age."

LeMay's military success and public relations catastrophes evolved from a frank . . . but ultimately realistic assessment of human and hence national behavior. "In all candor the strong and the rich are seldom popular. . . . Unless we start to win the wars we get into, we may find ourselves overextended around the world on several fronts. . . . To maintain such vast military forces America would become an armed camp with all our sons being drafted for these endless foreign wars. God forbid!"

Victor Davis Hanson, *The Cold War: A Military History.* New York: Random House, 2005, pp. 243, 259.

The launch of the Soviet satellite Sputnik *in October 1954 pushed the United States to make its own space program a priority, thus introducing another dimension to the Cold War competition between the two superpowers.*

trained an army of Guatemalan rebels in nearby Honduras and Nicaragua to launch a coup against Arbenz Guzmán, who resigned on June 27.

In Asia the United States became involved in the former French colony of Vietnam. The French had lost a bitter war with the Communists in 1954, and the colony was divided into North and South Vietnam. The United States provided matériel and financial support to South Vietnam, which was combating an insurgency from the Communist North. America's ability to prop up the South Vietnamese government was made more difficult by the citizens' lack of confidence in their president, Ngo Dinh Diem.

America's overseas commitments became widespread during Eisenhower's

presidency. Defense pacts and bilateral security agreements linked the United States to nations on every continent. Historian Ronald E. Powaski writes, "By 1958, the United States had assumed the explicit obligation of defending some forty-five countries and, by implication, several more."[34] It seemed as if there was no territory on Earth that did not measure some form of attention from the U.S. State Department or the U.S. military.

The Space Race

The contest for supremacy between America and the Soviet Union was so great that it could not be held to the earth itself. Both countries were dedicated to the conquest of space and put their best scientific minds to work on building rockets that could propel humans into orbit. The potentials for scientific achievement and the adventure in exploring unknown frontiers captivated the scientists and astronauts involved in America's space program. However, the desire to stay one step ahead of the Soviets and the military applications of the new space technology also motivated the U.S. government to continue funding.

Americans were proud of the nation's accumulated scientific and technical knowledge, and they felt particularly suited to the space program. That pride suffered a tremendous blow on October 4, 1957, when the Soviets were the first to launch a satellite into orbit. *Sputnik* (Russian for "Fellow Traveler"), measured 23 inches (58cm) in diameter, weighed 184 pounds (84kg), and emitted a beeping radio signal that could be heard on American radios when it passed overhead.

Panic swept over America. If Soviet rockets could reach space, then they could surely reach the United States with nuclear weapons. Democrats blamed Eisenhower for allowing Russia to take such a commanding lead in space exploration, but the president remained convinced that the United States would soon recover. America's well-publicized response, the launch of *Vanguard 1* on December 6, exploded after getting less than 5 feet (1.5m) off the launch pad. Critics dubbed the accident "flopnik."

America succeeded in putting a satellite called *Explorer 1* into space on January 31, 1958. It was much smaller than the Soviet satellites that preceded it, and Khrushchev teased that it was nothing more than a "grapefruit." The *Explorer* satellite provided much more scientific data than *Sputnik*, giving comfort to Americans that although the United States may not have been first into space, it was building a better space program. The creation of the National Aeronautics and Space Administration (NASA) on July 29 ensured the space program as a permanent fixture in American life. Within a decade, NASA had a $5 billion budget and thirty-six thousand employees.

Duck and Cover: American Culture in the 1950s

Soviet developments like *Sputnik* and the hydrogen bomb and the fear of nuclear war had a profound impact on the American people. Rational concern over the spread of communism sometimes gave

A family relaxes inside their steel underground radiation fallout shelter, complete with bunks and supplies. In the 1950s many American families installed fallout shelters in their backyards in order to protect themselves in the event of a nuclear attack.

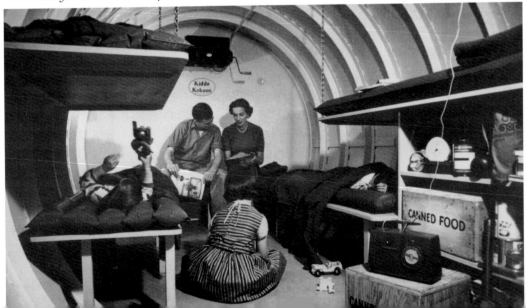

way to irrational fears that Communists were everywhere. There was nothing irrational, however, about fear of a war that would destroy civilization as each country built and tested bigger nuclear bombs.

Popular media of the time reflected these concerns in various ways. George Orwell's book *1984* illustrated the bleak lives of people living under oppressive governments. The science-fiction film *Invasion of the Body Snatchers* depicted aliens taking over peoples' bodies and turning them into unfeeling drones, which was meant to be symbolic of the effects of communism. Nevil Shute's novel *On the Beach* depicts the lonely days after a nuclear war in which the world's remaining survivors wait to die of radiation poisoning.

Not all of the entertainment was this bleak or unforgiving. Writer Mickey Spillane became one of the most popular authors of the twentieth century with a series of adult-oriented detective thrillers in which the hero, Mike Hammer, wins the upper hand over Communist spies and sympathizers. Ian Fleming, a former British intelligence operative, wrote a series of novels about the exploits of secret agent James Bond as he protects the world against evildoers. The books were translated into a popular series of films that endure to this day.

Heroes on film and in print could not protect the public from nuclear war. The U.S. government developed evacuation plans and survival strategies to help people cope with the frightful possibility of a nuclear attack. The Interstate Highway Act of 1956 established funding for the creation of a national system of highways that would facilitate the orderly evacuation of cities and the movement of

Schoolchildren participate in a classroom "duck and cover" drill in the 1950s, practicing the crouching position recommended by the Federal Civil Defense Administration to help them survive a nuclear attack.

The Superbomb

Throughout the 1950s the United States and the Soviet Union experimented with ever-larger nuclear weapons. These devices were often not practical weapons because they were so large they either had to be assembled on-site or delivered by slow-moving cargo planes that would be easily shot down in time of war. Despite their impracticality as weapons of war, these large nuclear bombs served as propaganda designed to demonstrate their nuclear and technical superiority.

This propaganda reached its limits on October 30, 1961, when the Soviets detonated a fifty-seven-megaton nuclear device in the Arctic. Author Gerard J. DeGroot explains:

The flash could be seen 1,000 kilometers (620 miles) away. . . . The mushroom cloud rose to sixty-four kilometers (40 miles), and the [shock wave] orbited the earth three times.

In clear air, the bomb would theoretically have been capable of inflicting third degree burns to a person standing 100 kilometers (62 miles) distant. . . . Such a weapon could cause complete destruction of all structures within a radius of twenty-five kilometers (15 miles), and severe damage to most construction within thirty-five kilometers (21 miles).

The bomb, nicknamed "Tsar Bomba," weighed 20 tons (18 metric tons) and was delivered by a retrofitted Soviet bomber. It was dropped by parachute so that the plane had enough time to reach a safe distance before the bomb detonated.

Gerard J. DeGroot, *The Bomb: A Life.* Cambridge, MA: Harvard University Press, 2005, p. 253.

military personnel in the event of a nuclear attack. The Federal Civil Defense Administration, established in 1949, gave guidance to American city planners to build and stock fallout shelters. Historians Jeremy Isaacs and Taylor Downing write, "Soon, the yellow-and-blue fallout shelter symbol could be seen in every city of the land. Americans could even buy their own private family fallout shelters, which magazines advertised at $2,395—installation extra."[35]

Children and adults were instructed that the best way to survive a nuclear explosion was to duck down when they saw the bright flash, face away from the blast, and cover their heads. This advice was highly ineffective considering that nuclear explosions could melt steel and topple buildings. The civil defense manuals of the 1950s did not mention how to deal with the massive number of casualties, the burn and radiation victims, the blind, and the mentally affected. There was also no

Outpost Mission

One of the Cold War's most closely guarded secrets was the plan to protect the president of the United States from a nuclear attack. It was revealed in Time *magazine in 1992.*

The project was known simply as the Outpost Mission. Beginning in the mid-1950s, an elite unit of helicopter pilots and crew was stationed at Olmsted Air Force Base in Pennsylvania posing as a rescue team for military and civilians in distress. Their real mission . . . was to rescue President Dwight D. Eisenhower—and, later, John F. Kennedy, Lyndon Johnson and Richard Nixon—in the event of a nuclear attack. . . . They were to swoop down onto the White House lawn when an attack seemed imminent and spirit the President away to one of several hollowed-out mountain sites or to the heavily reinforced communications ship, the U.S.S. Northampton, off the Atlantic Coast.

The pilots were also ready to make a rescue attempt after a nuclear assault. . . . They packed decontamination kits as well as crowbars and acetylene torches to break through the walls of the presidential bunker buried beneath the White House. . . . In the 1960s the squadron was moved to Dover Air Force Base in Delaware, and remained operational until 1970.

Outpost Mission was but a fragment of a vast and secret doomsday plan . . . to ensure the survival of the U.S. government, preserve order and salvage the economy in the aftermath of an atomic attack. Still others were charged with rescuing the nation's cultural heritage, from the Declaration of Independence to the priceless masterpieces of the National Gallery of Art.

Ted Gup and J. Guadalupe Carney, "The Doomsday Blueprints," *Time,* August 10, 1992. http://www.time.com/time/magazine/article/0,91,71,976187,00html.

mention of nuclear winter, the phenomenon in which large amounts of dust and smoke from a nuclear war would block out the sun, lower temperatures, and kill plant and animal life around the world.

The civil defense strategies of the 1950s would not save many lives in a nuclear war, but the suggestion of safety kept many people from panic. The developments in missile and weapons technology meant that the only defense in a nuclear war was not to let one happen in the first place. Unfortunately, the continued expansion of the Communist threat and the American commitment to meet it made nuclear war a greater possibility.

Chapter Four

The Success and Failure of Flexible Response

"Let every nation know, whether it wishes us well or ill, that we shall pay any price, bear any burden, meet any hardship, support any friend, oppose any foe to assure the survival and success of liberty."
—John F. Kennedy, January 20, 1961, inaugural address

Richard Nixon was considered an able successor to Eisenhower in the 1960 presidential election, but the wisdom of massive retaliation as a means of combating and containing communism came into question. Democratic senator John F. Kennedy argued that the threat of massive attack by the United States did not stop the Soviets from expanding their presence in Asia nor did it prevent the island nation of Cuba from becoming a Communist dictatorship 90 miles (145km) off the coast of Florida, which happened in 1959.

Kennedy narrowly defeated Nixon in the election, but the lack of widespread public support did not stop him from making significant changes in how America dealt with the Soviets. General Maxwell D. Taylor, a top adviser to Kennedy, recommended that the policy of massive retaliation be scrapped. He wrote that it "could offer our leaders only two choices: the initiation of general nuclear war, or compromise and retreat."[36] Taylor recommended replacing it with the doctrine of flexible response, which meant that each military challenge by the Soviets would be met based on its own conditions and its potential impact on U.S. interests.

Flexible response, which called for the large, conventional military that Eisenhower avoided, seemed to offer more options to the president in fighting the Cold War. This new strategy, like all the foreign policy strategies that preceded it, required a sincere understanding of what was in America's best interests. When those interests were clear, flexible response worked; however, when those interests appeared conflicted or confused, flexible response fell apart.

A Rocky Start for a New Leader

One clear illustration of the shift in popular American thinking as the country entered the 1960s was the fact that voters had turned control of the nation over from its oldest president to the youngest ever elected. Kennedy's youth represented a fresh perspective for many younger citizens hopeful for a more peaceful future, but the age of the new president did not change the dangers that existed beyond America's borders. If anything, leaders in Moscow took Kennedy's youth for inexperience and became emboldened in their efforts to stir worldwide Communist revolution.

Khrushchev noted in a January 6, 1961, speech that the Soviet Union would support wars of national liberation around the world, indicating that there would be more Communist insurgencies. Kennedy wanted to improve relations with the Soviets, but Khrushchev's speech and his specific mentions of Cuba and Vietnam alarmed the new president. Kennedy authorized a continued military buildup, adding more army divisions, naval vessels, tactical aircraft, and nuclear weapons to America's formidable arsenal.

The Central Intelligence Agency presented Kennedy with an opportunity to turn back the Soviet advance in Cuba with plans for an invasion that had been developed in the final months of Eisenhower's administration. The plan called

Cuban leader Fidel Castro, center, talks to his troops near the site of the Bay of Pigs invasion in April 1961.

for Cuban exiles to land at the Bay of Pigs on the island's south coast with American air support, stir up a popular revolt, and overthrow the Communist dictatorship of Fidel Castro.

Kennedy supported the operation, but he was concerned that America's involvement would lead to an escalation of tensions with the Soviets. Shortly before the invasion, he cut air support. Alert Communist militia stopped the anti-Castro exiles on the beach. Many of the exiles were killed in the fighting or were captured and later executed. Kennedy later confessed to Eisenhower that he withdrew wider American support for fear of a Soviet counterattack in Berlin. Eisenhower disagreed: "If [the Soviets] see us show any weakness, that is when they press us hardest. The second they see us show strength . . . that is when they are very cagey."[37]

The Berlin Wall

No symbol of the Cold War was more prominent than the 96-mile-long (155km) concrete barrier that divided East and West Berlin from 1961 until 1989. The Berlin Wall began as a barbed-wire barricade on August 13, 1961, to stanch the flight of East German citizens to the West. Historian Frederick Taylor writes about the late-night border-sealing operation:

Sentries were placed at two-meter (6.5ft) intervals along the entire Berlin sector border to prevent escapes, while border troops, factory paramilitaries and construction units barricaded the streets by means of barbed wire, tank traps and improvised concrete bolsters. Streetlights were turned off, masking the nature of the operation. . . .

All 193 streets that straddled the border would be closed. Twelve underground and surface city railway lines were to be blocked off at the sector borders. Dozens of stations on or near the border were to be closed and sealed.

The barbed wire was replaced by a 12-foot-high (3.6m) concrete wall that was modified continuously after 1965 with trip wires, mesh fencing that made it difficult to climb, and watchtowers.

By the time the wall came down in 1989, eighty-six people had lost their lives attempting to escape East Berlin. Some five thousand successful escapes were made during the twenty-eight years that the Berlin Wall divided the city through numerous methods, including hot-air balloons, sliding along aerial wires, and flying gliders over the checkpoints.

Frederick Taylor, *The Berlin Wall: A World Divided, 1961–1989.* New York: HarperCollins, 2006, p. 162.

East German troops use barbed wire to create a barricade between Berlin's eastern and western sectors in August 1961, the start of what eventually became a permanent structure known as the Berlin Wall.

The failure at the Bay of Pigs dealt Kennedy a significant political blow. Congressmen and military figures who were distrustful of him initially were now convinced he lacked the courage to back up his tough words against communism. Khrushchev believed that he could make harsh demands of the beleaguered president and get essentially whatever he wanted.

When the two leaders met in Vienna for a summit on June 3, Kennedy was at a disadvantage. Khrushchev had a reputation for being tough, boisterous, and even belligerent with foreign leaders. He was very adamant about obtaining new concessions with regard to Berlin, including a complete American withdrawal from the city by the end of 1961. Kennedy refused to concede to such a demand because it would signal America's inability to maintain its security commitments elsewhere. Khrushchev threatened dire consequences, to which Kennedy responded, "If that's true, then it's going to be a cold winter."[38]

U.S. and Soviet forces remained in a standoff in Berlin for the rest of the summer, during which time the East German military erected a wall between the German and American sectors of the city to prevent people from fleeing to the West. The crisis fizzled out without Khrushchev ever admitting defeat, but it was the last time America would be pressed to withdraw from the divided city of Berlin. However, it was not the last time that Kennedy and Khrushchev would come close to war.

To the Brink of Annihilation

Military advisers told Kennedy on October 16, 1962, that American spy flights revealed ballistic missile sites under construction in Cuba. There were at least sixteen, but possibly thirty-two, nuclear missiles with a 1,000-mile (1,609km)

A 1962 spy photo shows the presence of Soviet nuclear weapons and related equipment and structures at a ballistic missile base in Cuba, a discovery that brought the superpowers to the brink of war.

Department store workers and shoppers watch President John F. Kennedy's October 1962 speech informing Americans that Soviet missiles had been discovered in Cuba and that the United States was enacting a blockade of the island nation.

range on the island. Attorney General Robert Kennedy noted, "The estimate was that within a few minutes of their being fired, eighty million Americans would be dead."[39]

The United States could not accept such a bold move by the Soviets, nor could it tolerate being at such a strategic disadvantage. Kennedy pulled together a group of top military and political advisers, known as the Executive Committee. They met in secret over the next several days because they did not want the Soviets to know they were aware of the missile sites until they had prepared a sufficient response. U.S. forces around the world positioned themselves on high alert, and troops, artillery, and air-

craft were moved to Florida. Strategic bombers were dispersed around the country, and naval vessels poured into the Caribbean and the Gulf of Mexico.

Kennedy made a televised speech on October 22 announcing the presence of offensive missiles in Cuba. Kennedy called the establishment of the missile sites so close to the United States "a deliberately provocative and unjustified change in the status quo which cannot be accepted by this country if our courage and our commitments are ever to be trusted again by either friend or foe."[40] He announced a blockade of Cuba until construction was halted and the missiles were removed.

The next several days were extremely tense for Americans and much of the world. Construction of the missile sites continued, as did the U.S. and Soviet military buildups in the Caribbean and Europe. There appeared to be no avoiding war. Martin Walker illustrates just how certain people were convinced that the end was near:

At a retrospective discussion of the crisis in Moscow in March 1988, the then US Defense Secretary Robert McNamara spoke of . . . Saturday, 27 October [1962]. . . . "It was a beautiful fall evening, the height of the crisis, and I went up into the open air to look and to smell it, because I thought it was the last Saturday I would ever see." Fyodor Burlatsky, who had been one of Khrushchev's advisers in the crisis, went pale. "That was when I went and telephoned my wife and told her to drop everything and get out of Moscow. I thought your bombers were on the way."[41]

Khrushchev proposed removing the missiles if Kennedy promised not to invade Cuba and to remove nuclear missiles from Turkey. A small battery of American missiles had been placed in Turkey during the Eisenhower administration, but they were considered obsolete and were about to be removed anyway. The Soviets did not know this; they only knew that the removal of the missiles from Turkey seemed like a fair exchange for the removal of missiles from Cuba. Kennedy accepted the deal, but the provision regarding the Turkish missiles was kept secret for several years.

The Cuban Missile Crisis was the closest the United States had come to engaging in a nuclear war with the Soviets since the Cold War began. Kennedy successfully negotiated the country through the crisis, but military leaders like U.S. Air Force chief of staff Curtis LeMay believed that America came out of the crisis as losers. To them, the opportunity to rid Cuba of Castro and defeat the Soviets had slipped away, only to be delayed to another time when America might not have such a distinct advantage.

As a direct result of the crisis, a Washington-Moscow hotline was installed, allowing the leaders in Washington and the Kremlin to talk directly over the phone in moments of crisis. The Atmospheric Test Ban Treaty of August 5, 1963, prevented the testing of nuclear weapons in the atmosphere, in space, and underwater. It was the first formal agreement between the United States and the USSR to control nuclear activities.

Escalation in Vietnam

Efforts at greater communication between the superpowers signaled hope for a more stable world, but the contest for supremacy in global affairs continued. In Southeast Asia, the United States had been sending money and matériel support to the South Vietnamese government in its fight with an aggressive Communist insurgency led by the Vietcong, guerrilla fighters from North Vietnam who were backed by the Soviets.

America had a great deal of difficulty making progress in Vietnam in part because the corrupt South Vietnamese government could not even draw the support of its own people. There appeared to be a widespread unwillingness to fight for their own freedom, and the burden of the battle slowly transferred over to the Americans. After the French defeat in 1954, many American politicians suspected that South Vietnam was a lost cause. Even Kennedy, a senator at the time, said, "To pour money, materiel, and men into the jungles of [Vietnam] without at least a remote prospect of victory would be dangerously futile and self-destructive."[42]

As president, Kennedy apparently thought quite differently. Between 1961 and 1963, U.S. military advisers in Vietnam increased from seven hundred to sixteen thousand. The role of the advisers expanded as well. Kennedy publicly denied that they were engaged in combat, but American military personnel in Vietnam were commanding South Vietnamese troops under fire and assisting them in covert actions.

Kennedy threatened to withdraw support from President Diem unless he ended corruption and stopped oppressing the Buddhist minority, but he knew that the South Vietnamese did not stand a chance against the Vietcong without American support. He was also motivated by deeper political considerations. Kennedy had numerous critics who believed he was soft on communism because he failed to remove Castro from Cuba on two occasions. He did not want

U.S. troops evacuate from a Vietcong position in December 1965. By then, the number of American soldiers deployed to assist South Vietnam in combating a Communist insurgency led by guerrilla fighters from the north topped 184,000.

Francis Gary Powers

Francis Gary Powers was a U.S. Air Force pilot who joined the CIA in 1956 to fly reconnaissance missions over the Soviet Union. The aircraft of choice for such missions was the Lockheed U-2, a single-engine aircraft that flew at high altitudes and was difficult to track by radar. These qualities, and Powers's skill as a pilot, helped him avoid being shot down by the Soviets for violating their airspace on numerous occasions. On May 1, 1960, Powers was sent on a mission to view a Soviet missile range. Norman Friedman describes what happened next:

A Soviet missile shot Powers down near Sverdlovsk. The flimsy U-2 was sometimes described as a jet-powered glider. Eisenhower was assured that Powers had been killed and the airplane destroyed. Khrushchev produced not only a live Powers (who later said he was shot down because his airplane descended too low) but also cameras and developed film.

Powers was convicted of espionage and was sentenced to three years in prison and seven years of hard labor, but he was released to the United States in exchange for a Soviet spy in 1962. Some criticized him for not taking the cyanide that all U-2 pilots were given in case of capture; he was also criticized for failing to engage his plane's self-destruct mechanism. A congressional investigation found that Powers acted competently in dangerous circumstances.

Powers died in a helicopter crash in 1977 while working as a pilot for KNBC television news in Los Angeles. He was posthumously awarded the Distinguished Flying Cross, the National Defense Service Medal, and the Prisoner of War Medal.

Norman Friedman, *The Fifty-Year War: Conflict and Strategy in the Cold War.* Annapolis, MD: Naval Institute, 2000, p. 239.

U.S. Air Force pilot Francis Gary Powers, whose U-2 spy plane had been shot down over the Soviet Union, appears at his trial in Moscow in August 1960, where he was convicted of espionage.

to be seen as letting another country fall to the Communists.

Dramatic Changes East and West

Kennedy supported a coup in South Vietnam on November 2, 1963, in the hope that a change in leadership would improve the situation. Diem was deposed and murdered, even though Kennedy wanted a bloodless transition of power. The new leader, General Duong Van Minh, did not bring any stability to the situation. American military leaders considered him weak and stupid, and other South Vietnamese military leaders overthrew Minh several months later.

No one would ever know with any certainty how Kennedy would have handled the deteriorating situation in Vietnam. On November 22 he was assassinated as his motorcade passed through Dallas on the way to a speech. Lee Harvey Oswald, a lone Communist sympathizer who had lived in Russia from 1959 to 1962, was arrested for the crime, but he was killed on November 24, severely complicating the investigation into the president's murder. Although conspiracy theories continue to this day, no solid evidence ever surfaced that the Soviet government was involved in Kennedy's assassination.

Vice President Lyndon Johnson assumed the presidency upon Kennedy's death, and he continued to remain involved in Vietnam. He maintained the same staff of advisers, and he promised them, "I'm not going to be the president who saw Southeast Asia go the way China went."[43] The nuclear buildup also kept pace, with America closing out the 1960s with 1,059 intercontinental ballistic missiles (ICBMs), 700 submarine-launched ballistic missiles (SLBMs), and 500 B-52 bombers.

In 1964 Nikita Khrushchev was deposed as head of the Soviet Union after losing favor with the Kremlin for his performance during the Cuban Missile Crisis. Leonid Brezhnev replaced him, and the Soviets engaged in a nuclear buildup of their own that exceeded the expectations of American intelligence estimates. By 1969 they had 1,028 ICBMs when the United States expected them to have no more than 700.

Mired in Southeast Asia

Johnson followed the strategy of flexible response that Kennedy had embraced, but he applied it incorrectly in Vietnam. Flexible response meant applying force equivalent to America's interests, which meant that the goal that was stated had to justify the means by which that goal was achieved. Johnson knew that his goal was to prevent South Vietnam from falling to the Communists, but he did not recognize the high price that had to be paid in order to achieve that goal.

Johnson continued to boost troop levels, with American soldiers in Vietnam numbering 184,000 by the end of 1965. Tens of thousands more U.S. Air Force and naval personnel were also stationed in the region, along with thousands of civilian advisers and military contractors. By 1966 more than 7,500 Americans had been killed in Vietnam, yet the Vietcong insurgency actually increased over

Unrest in the Dominican Republic

While the world's attention was focused on America's intervention in Vietnam in 1965, American soldiers were engaged in a battle with leftist forces in the Dominican Republic. Operation Power Pack was the code name given to the mission to protect American civilians caught in the crossfire of civil strife that erupted after a Communist military coup displaced the island nation's civilian government on April 24, 1965. Author Richard K. Kolb defines the situation:

Shoved into this highly sensitive situation were, at the peak of the intervention, 20,463 U.S. forces (12,439 soldiers, 6,924 Marines and 1,100 airmen) with an additional 10,059 sailors offshore. . . .

Some 40 U.S. vessels . . . cordoned off the island. The carrier USS Okinawa . . . was among the ships. . . .

The backbone of Power Pack was the 82nd Airborne Division—the "fire brigade" of the nation's strategic reserve. Its three brigades fielded nine airborne infantry battalions.

American troops defended themselves against fierce opposition from the rebels while peace talks brought sporadic cease-fires that only U.S. troops honored. Eventually the conflict subsided, and in June 1966 elections put a new government in place and American troops went home.

The intervention had cost the U.S. 27 [killed in action] and 172 [wounded in action]. . . . Another 20 Americans died from other causes; 111 were seriously injured.

Intervention, in this case, succeeded. The civil war was stopped, stability restored and transition to democratic government assured. Graffiti on city walls said it all: "Yankee go home—and take me with you."

Richard K. Kolb, "Cold War Along the 'Cactus Curtain,'" *VFW Magazine*, January 1999.

---

this time. The strategy of graduated pressure, which meant a steady heightening of American military action against the North Vietnamese, had no effect on their ability to fight.

Several factors worked against the Americans in Vietnam, many of which became evident only after years of fighting. Johnson insisted on running the war himself, and he personally chose bombing targets and attack strategies, yet he had no military background to justify his level of involvement in war planning. His concern about escalating the war and drawing Russia and China directly into the conflict meant that American forces had to strictly limit their rules of engagement with an enemy that was not equally inhibited. The South Vietnamese government went through several rulers, each one sapping the morale of citizens who saw no difference between their ineffective leaders and the Communists. Additionally, American troops had never fought a guerrilla conflict in a jungle environment with an elusive enemy, and many unskilled soldiers lost their lives as a result.

The futility of the conflict became clear on January 30, 1968, when eighty thousand North Vietnamese troops launched a massive offensive across South Vietnam during the Tet New Year holiday. The Tet Offensive, like much of the war, played out on American television screens as North Vietnamese troops swarmed into Saigon and battled with U.S. troops on the grounds of the American embassy. After eight weeks American and South Vietnamese troops beat back the offensive, with the U.S. suffering thirty-eight hundred casualties, but morale in the United States had been shattered. After some twenty-five thousand dead soldiers and $80 billion in military spending, the United States appeared no closer to victory in Vietnam than when it first started sending advisers in the late 1950s. The American public had had enough.

Discord in America

Johnson's popularity plummeted after Tet, and on March 31, 1968, he announced that he would not seek reelection. He had hoped to stall the spread of communism in Asia, but in hoping to do so with minimal political risk, he failed

Delegates to the 1968 Democratic National Convention in Chicago, Illinois, denounce the country's involvement in the Vietnam War, as did a growing number of Americans in the late 1960s, many of whom expressed their sentiments in protests and riots throughout the country.

miserably. The injection of politics into the management of the war made it seem political rather than patriotic to the American public, and therefore not worth the price of American lives.

Different protest movements on American university campuses and in urban centers over civil rights and class and racial disparity united over their hatred of the Vietnam War. The original goal of containing communism in Vietnam did not matter to the younger generation that had grown up in affluent America. They were not old enough to recall the repression of Eastern Europe and much of Asia by the Communists. In their view, the U.S. government was the greater purveyor of violence in Southeast Asia. The urban poor, mostly blacks and Hispanics, despised the war because they thought it unfair that they be drafted to fight to defend American freedoms that they did not share at home. Riots broke out in major cities across the country, causing billions of dollars in property damage.

Politicians also began speaking out openly against the war. Robert Kennedy became the likely Democratic nominee for president in 1968 on his promise to end the war, but he was assassinated in June. The Democratic convention in Chicago in August became a focal point for antiwar protesters. Vice President Hubert Humphrey's nomination as the Democratic candidate for president was overshadowed by the street battles between police and demonstrators, which resulted in many injuries and arrests.

Republican candidate Richard Nixon promised to end the war by bringing peace with honor to America. He disagreed with the manner in which it had been fought, noting, "Never has so much military and economic and diplomatic power been used so ineffectively."[44] He defeated Humphrey in the November election and set about a complicated strategy to withdraw from Vietnam while preserving American prestige. Nixon was perhaps the staunchest anti-Communist still active in American politics, and his presence in the White House meant that the United States was headed for yet another change in policy in its relations with the Soviet Union.

Chapter Five

A New Approach

"I don't know why you use a fancy French word like detente when there's a good English phrase for it—cold war."
—Israeli prime minister Golda Meir

America's involvement in Vietnam started out as an attempt to stem the tide of Communist aggression, much like America had done in Korea, Europe, the Middle East, and Latin America. Vietnam ended up becoming a military and foreign policy failure that America had never experienced before in its history. The high price paid in lives and money to save a foreign land from Communist infiltration that few had heard of before 1964 forced many people to reevaluate the very nature of America's role in a world that was becoming an ever more dangerous place.

By the time Nixon became president in 1969, thirty-one thousand Americans had died in Vietnam. America's allies in Europe had become similarly disillusioned with U.S. involvement in the war, believing that it distracted the country from its European commitments. The Soviets had achieved a level of nuclear firepower equal to that of the United States. Long-festering political and ideological disagreements between the Soviets and the Chinese were pushing the Communist giants toward war. Many leaders and citizens around the world saw civilization heading toward chaos. Nixon and his national security adviser, Henry Kissinger, saw an opportunity for a more stable world order.

Nixon and Kissinger engaged in a strategy that both men felt accurately reflected America's strategic goals and its national interests. It would require a fundamental change in the thinking of the time. As Kissinger explained it, "We have no permanent enemies . . . we will judge other countries, including communist countries . . . on the basis of their actions and not on the basis of their domestic ideology."[45] It was a bold strategy, but before it could take place America had to get out of Vietnam.

Searching for Peace with Honor

Nixon knew that getting America out of Vietnam would be a complex task. The U.S. troop withdrawal could not be perceived as a cut-and-run operation. America would lose the respect of its allies, and the Soviets would be emboldened by its perceived lack of resolve. Nixon wanted South Vietnam to be left with a fighting chance to defend itself against the North Vietnamese insurgency. At the same time, he had to clearly demonstrate to impatient domestic critics that America was winding down its commitment in Vietnam.

Coup in Chile

In 1970 Salvador Allende Gossens was elected president of Chile, enacting a Socialist agenda and nationalizing American-owned businesses. This, plus the support he received from Cuba's dictator, Fidel Castro, caused great concern with the U.S. government. The CIA supported labor strikes by Allende's opponents and negative media coverage of Allende, who was accused of ignoring Chile's constitution and court decisions.

On September 11, 1973, General Augusto Pinochet led a coup to overthrow Allende. National security adviser Henry Kissinger describes what happened next:

Opposition radio stations broadcast a proclamation by the commanders-in-chief of the army, air force, and national police and the chief of naval operations calling on President Allende to resign. The commanders declared that the armed forces and the police were united in their fight against Marxism and against an incompetent government that was leading the country to chaos.

On nationwide radio [Allende] refused to resign. . . . After the air force bombed the Presidential Palace, army troops entered it around noon. They found Allende dead. Our embassy conveyed to Washington the report that he had committed suicide, apparently with a submachine gun that had been a gift from Fidel Castro.

The government of Pinochet that followed Allende remained allied to the United States, but it was tainted by corruption and the harsh treatment of political opponents. Thousands of people disappeared during Pinochet's rule and were presumed killed, while thousands more were tortured or exiled for their opposition of Pinochet.

Henry Kissinger, *Years of Upheaval*. Boston: Little, Brown, 1982, p. 404.

North Vietnamese leaders were not eager to negotiate a settlement. They wanted nothing less than the complete withdrawal of U.S. forces, a halt to the American bombing campaign, and a right to choose their own destiny in Vietnam, which ultimately meant taking over South Vietnam and uniting the two nations into one Communist country. They held the upper hand because they knew that America was leaving Vietnam. They merely had to wait until the United States left to get what they wanted.

America's weak bargaining position was clearly illustrated by the phased troop withdrawal that began in the summer of 1969, reducing American forces from 540,000 to 425,000 by the end of the year. An additional 91,000 troops were pulled out in 1970, and by 1971 American forces were reduced to 156,000. During this time, U.S. military advisers were training and equipping South Vietnamese soldiers to take on a larger combat role. As Kissinger explained it, "We would be in a race between the decline in our combat capability and the improvement of South Vietnamese forces."[46] The end result was a fighting force that was low on morale and outmatched by the battle-hardened North Vietnamese.

In order to soften the North Vietnamese bargaining position and allow the South Vietnamese a better fighting position, Nixon authorized a controversial bombing campaign in 1969 that went after North Vietnamese supply bases in nearby Laos and Cambodia. The bombing caused angry protests in America from people claiming that Nixon was actually expanding the war rather than ending it as he promised. In 1970 the Cooper-Church Amendment was added to the Senate defense spending bill, prohibiting American forces from operating in Laos and Cambodia.

Nixon still had options available to him. He turned to Russia and China in separate secret talks, hoping to use their influence over North Vietnam to force a settlement. It was ironic that America was turning to China and the Soviet Union to help it withdraw from a conflict it entered into to prevent the spread of Chinese and Soviet influence in Asia. It turned out that neither the Soviets nor the Chinese had as much influence over the North Vietnamese as Nixon suspected, but they were open to negotiating with the United States because of their mutual distrust for each other.

Détente

Relations between the Soviet Union and Communist China had been deteriorating throughout the 1960s. The Soviet Union had traditionally seen itself as the premier Communist state, with all other Communist nations subordinate to its rule. The Chinese Communists under Mao Zedong did not feel beholden to the Soviets for the comparatively small amount of aid they received over the years.

Leonid Brezhnev's ruthless defeat of a revolt in the Soviet satellite state of Czechoslovakia in 1968 led the Chinese to believe that Russia might deal with them in a similar manner. Skirmishes along the common border of the two countries had increased in intensity, leaving an unknown

number of dead soldiers on both sides. Troop buildups and missile deployments in 1969 indicated that war seemed imminent.

Nixon began taking steps for better relations with the Chinese shortly after taking office because he suspected they might be looking for an ally in their dealings with the Soviets. It also figured into his broader plan to ease tensions with the Communist bloc. He had written two years earlier, "We simply cannot afford to leave China forever outside the family of nations. . . . There is no place on this small planet for a billion of its potentially most able people to live in angry isolation."[47]

The American travel ban to Communist China was lifted, and the trade embargo was eased. Nixon also ended naval patrols of the Taiwan Strait. Kissinger

met secretly in Beijing with Mao and Premier Chou En-Lai in July 1971 and discussed relations between the two countries. Nixon and Kissinger did much of the early diplomatic work with China in secret because they feared the bureaucracy of the U.S. State Department would fumble a historic opportunity.

Nixon traveled to China from February 21 through 28, 1972. He walked along the Great Wall, he shook hands with Mao, and he was toasted by Chou in the Great Hall of the People in Beijing. Formal diplomatic ties were established between the two nations, and Nixon pledged to allow China to peacefully settle its differences with Taiwan, which China still regarded as a renegade province.

Recognizing "Red China" was a bold move for any U.S. president, but Nixon was better suited than anyone to reach out to Mao. His lifelong reputation as a strong anti-Communist insulated him from charges of being soft on communism. He could also afford to deemphasize ideology as the driving force of American foreign policy because the Soviet-Chinese split proved that there was no international unity among Communist countries. Each nation, democratic or Communist, was operating in its own best interests.

The Soviets recognized that it was in their best interest to soften relations with the United States in the wake of Nixon's trip to China. Just as the Chinese welcomed American diplomatic relations in order to offset their conflict with the Soviets, the USSR wanted better relations with the United States because it did not want to face a hostile China allied with America.

Nixon visited Russia from May 22 through 30, 1972, for a historic meeting with Brezhnev. Shortly before the meeting was to take place, concerns arose that the Soviets would cancel the summit. The United States had engaged in a massive bombing campaign of military targets in North Vietnam in response to a Communist offensive launched on March 30. The summit went on as scheduled, however. One Soviet diplomat told the *Washington Post*, "We've done a lot for those Vietnamese, but we're not going to let them spoil our relations with the United States."[48]

Nixon and Brezhnev signed the Strategic Arms Limitation Talks (SALT) agreement on May 26, which limited the development and construction of land- and sea-based nuclear missiles by both nations. The SALT agreement did not reduce the number of missiles that currently existed, but it did attempt to freeze the current balance in place. An additional Anti-Ballistic Missile (ABM) Treaty was signed that severely restricted the construction of missile defense systems. This agreement was born of Soviet concerns that American advances in antimissile technology would render their missiles obsolete, thereby

President Richard Nixon and Soviet leader Leonid Brezhnev shake hands in May 1972 after the signing of the Strategic Arms Limitation Talks (SALT) agreement at the Moscow Summit.

upsetting the balance of MAD and making nuclear war more likely.

Russia and China did not provide any substantial help to the United States in withdrawing from Vietnam. American bombing campaigns that devastated military targets in North Vietnam were what led directly to the signing of an armistice in Paris on January 27, 1973. Nixon's plan for a more stable world order, referred to as détente, or an easing of relations, had worked. He explained his concept in 1972: "The only time in the history of the world that we have had any extended period of peace is when there has been a balance of power. It is when one nation becomes infinitely more powerful in relation to its potential competitors that the danger of war arises."[49]

American Power Falters

Nixon was reelected in 1972 by the largest margin in American history at that time. His landslide election was based in large part on his foreign policy successes. America's withdrawal from Vietnam had been achieved, but at the price of fifty-nine thousand dead. The scars of the first major military defeat in the country's history would take years to heal. The mood in the country grew even darker as it became evident that Nixon was involved in a cover-up of the June 1972 burglary of the Democratic National Committee headquarters at the Watergate office complex in Washington, D.C. The scandal ultimately led to Nixon's resignation on August 9, 1974.

Vice President Gerald Ford then became president. Ford attempted to hold the line against Communist aggression, but he faced a hostile Congress that wanted no part of international commitments that could potentially cost American lives. The momentum of foreign policy successes that Nixon achieved ended with his presidency.

In April 1975, as the North Vietnamese began their final offensive to conquer South Vietnam, Congress refused to provide military assistance to the South Vietnamese government. A series of resolutions also restricted U.S. intervention throughout Southeast Asia as Cambodia and Laos fell to the Communists. Millions were killed and displaced throughout Southeast Asia during the 1970s as brutal Communist dictatorships waged war against sovereign governments, civilians, and each other.

Congress also turned down requests by Ford to provide assistance to forces fighting a Communist insurgency in the African nation of Angola. The Soviet Union and Cuba provided full military and economic support, and the Communists took control of the country in 1976. Kissinger told Congress, "Angola represents the first time that the Soviets have moved militarily at long distance to impose a regime of their choice. It is the first time that the United States has failed to respond. . . . An ominous precedent has been set."[50]

America seemed reluctant to continue the fight against the Communists, and it did not have much money to fund the endeavor in any event. The Vietnam War and undisciplined domestic spending in the 1960s created a lack of faith in stock

Détente in Space: The *Apollo-Soyuz* Mission

America and the Soviet Union each viewed the other as a competitor in the conquest of space during the Cold War. Better relations on Earth led to a historic opportunity to work together in space as well during the Apollo-Soyuz Test Project (ASTP). After two years of joint planning between their space agencies, American astronauts and Soviet cosmonauts met in orbit in July 1975 to conduct scientific experiments and demonstrate the goodwill possible between the superpowers.

The Soviet Soyuz *and the American* Apollo *capsules were launched into orbit on July 15 and docked on July 17. The mission objectives are described on the NASA history Web site.*

Primary ASTP mission objectives were to evaluate the docking and undocking of an Apollo spacecraft with a Soyuz, and determine the adequacy of the onboard orientation lights and docking target; evaluate the ability of astronauts and cosmonauts to make inter-vehicular crew transfers and the ability of spacecraft systems to support the transfers: evaluate the Apollo's capability of maintaining attitude-hold control of the docked vehicles and performing attitude maneuvers; measure quantitatively the effect of weightlessness on the crews' height and lower limb volume, according to length of exposure to zero-g [zero gravity]; and obtain relay and direct synchronous-satellite navigation tracking data to determine their accuracy for application to Space Shuttle navigation-system design. The objectives were successfully completed, and the mission was adjudged successful.

After two days, the two capsules separated and returned to Earth, with the Soyuz *capsule landing on July 21 and the* Apollo *capsule landing on July 24.*

Charles Redmond, "The Flight of the Apollo-Soyuz," NASA History, October 22, 2004. http://history.nasa. gov/apollo/apsoyhist. html.

Soviet cosmonaut Alexei Leonov, left, joins American astronaut Deke Slayton in July 1975 after docking their respective capsules in space as part of a joint project between the superpowers to conduct a series of scientific experiments while in orbit.

and credit markets. Oil prices rose significantly as Arab oil-producing countries sought to punish America for its support of Israel during the 1967 and 1973 wars in which Arab countries tried to destroy the Jewish state. The resultant impact on the American economy was known as stagflation, in which both inflation and unemployment increased.

Less money led to smaller defense budgets and deep cuts in U.S. forces. The Army shrank by 200,000 soldiers, and throughout the decade only two new strategic weapons systems were developed. By contrast, the Soviets added 250,000 soldiers to their army and designed and deployed eight new types of intercontinental ballistic missiles and a long-range strategic bomber. Nixon was often accused by his critics of being a warmonger, but historian John Lewis Gaddis disagrees. "The Nixon-Ford years saw the most substantial reductions in American military capabilities relative to those of the Soviet Union in the entire postwar era."[51]

Détente Disintegrates

By the time Jimmy Carter, the former Democratic governor of Georgia, was elected president in 1976, many in Washington had lost faith in détente. America had surrendered its nuclear advantage with the SALT treaty, it had given up ABM defense development, and it was prepared to offer the Soviets historic trade concessions that would boost Russia's sagging economy. However, America's good faith was not returned in kind. Communism was on the march in Asia and

Africa, the Soviets were building bigger and better nuclear missiles, and a widespread crackdown on dissidents—Russians who spoke out against their government—was taking place in Russia.

Détente had very different meanings in the United States and the USSR. America interpreted détente as an easing of tensions with the Soviets that would allow the two nations to step back from the brink of war. For the Soviets, as military historian Norman Friedman notes, "permanently friendly relations meant that the United States would no longer oppose the world [Communist] revolution."[52] The Soviets believed that their arms buildup was finally paying off.

Carter did not recognize this, and he was keen on reviving détente through continued arms control agreements. He also placed a high value on human rights, which led to his public criticism of the Soviet Union in this area. This mixing of issues led to a slowdown in arms control talks. An internal Soviet memorandum to the Soviet ambassador in Washington on February 18, 1977, noted, "We firmly believe that the questions of domestic development that reflect the differences in ideologies and social political systems should not be the subject of inter-state relations."[53]

The confusion in Carter's messages came in large part from his complete lack of foreign policy experience. In addition, the two men whom he trusted most to guide him in foreign policy were often opposed in their views. Secretary of State Cyrus Vance believed that accommodation with the Soviets would produce

The Miracle at Lake Placid

The quadrennial Olympic Games were a scene of immense competition between the United States and the Soviet Union. Each nation sought to use the field of sports as proof that its way of life was superior to its opponent's. The Soviets took the Olympics quite seriously, cultivating young men and women for years under rigorous training conditions to produce unbeatable athletes.

The ice hockey team the Soviets sent to the 1980 Winter Olympics in Lake Placid, New York, was the world's best, having beaten all challengers, including all-stars from the National Hockey League. The U.S. hockey team, composed mostly of college and amateur players, was ranked seventh among the twelve teams that competed.

The two teams met on February 22 during the medal round with the Soviet team heavily favored to defeat the U.S. team and move on to the finals and the gold medal. The U.S. team played a superior game, defeating the Soviets 4–3. Contrary to popular belief, this was not the game that secured the gold medal for the U.S. team. That would come two days later against Finland. But sportswriter Kevin Allen explains why the U.S.–Soviet matchup is more celebrated:

Soviet players were Darth Vader on skates, unemotional soldiers from the evil empire. . . . Images of athletic Frankensteins created in laboratory experiments were conjured up. . . .

Remember, the American public of 1980 was disillusioned. Ayatollah Khomeini had kept Americans imprisoned for more than 100 days. The Soviets had invaded Afghanistan. At home, America faced domestic inflation, unemployment, and economic uncertainty. The United States didn't seem to be as mighty on the global scene as it once was—until its hockey team hit the ice.

That's why Americans loved the 1980 hockey team and their victory over the Soviets. They made America feel like it was back in control.

Kevin Allen, *USA Hockey: A Celebration of a Great Tradition.* Chicago: Triumph, 1997, p. 107.

Members of the American and Soviet Olympic hockey teams shake hands after the shocking U.S. medal-round victory in February 1980 known as the "Miracle on Ice."

better results, while national security adviser Zbigniew Brzezinski favored a tougher stance because accommodation had brought only more Soviet demands.

Each view had merit and had been practiced at various times during the Cold War, but it was not possible to pursue both methods simultaneously and get results. This only served to make American foreign policy appear confused and without direction, which was precisely the case during this point in time.

Carter was able to negotiate another nuclear arms control agreement, SALT II, which he and Brezhnev signed in Vienna, Austria, on June 18, 1979. Carter took the treaty back to the U.S. Senate for ratification, but he could draw little support for the agreement. Liberals accustomed to the idea that unilateral cuts in nuclear arms would lead to Soviet moderation felt the treaty did not go far enough. Conservatives felt the treaty went too far, and they embraced the view of defense secretary Harold Brown, who said, "We have found that when we build weapons, they build. When we stop, they nevertheless continue to build."[54]

The debate was finally settled, but it was done so by Soviet actions thousands of miles away. On December 25, 1979, the Soviet army invaded Afghanistan in an attempt to prop up a pro-Soviet regime. SALT II was dead, and American-Soviet relations hit a new low.

America at a Low Point

Carter expressed his anger over the Afghan invasion by announcing a grain embargo of the Soviet Union and by boycotting the 1980 Summer Olympics in Moscow. The boycott was a controversial move because no country had ever in-

The wreckage of a U.S. transport plane litters the desert after the failed April 1980 mission to rescue American hostages in Iran.

jected politics into the Olympics to such a degree. It was a move that also garnered little international support, as only Canada, Norway, Turkey, and West Germany followed the American example.

By and large, America's European allies had grown weary of the Cold War and had begun pursuing their own policies toward the Soviet Union in the 1970s. Western Europe was no longer willing to be on the front line of a nuclear standoff between the superpowers. Commitments to the North Atlantic Treaty Organization became secondary to domestic concerns, and accommodation with the Soviet Union became preferable to supporting American foreign policy.

Carter pushed for a hike in defense spending for 1980, but his firm resolve had come too late. Soviet backing of Arab nationalist groups led to a wave of terrorist organizations throughout the Middle East and North Africa dedicated to the destruction of Israel and America. Terrorist attacks became commonplace. In 1979 the shah of Iran was deposed in a Muslim fundamentalist revolution that placed the anti-American Ayatollah Ruholla Khomeini in power. On November 4, under Khomeini's orders, young Muslim radicals seized control of the American embassy and held fifty-two Americans hostage for 444 days.

Carter ordered a covert rescue attempt codenamed Eagle Claw to rescue the hostages. The mission was aborted when a helicopter collided with a transport plane at the final staging area in Iran, killing eight American soldiers. With the help of Algerian diplomats, a deal was eventually made in which the United States promised nonintervention in Iranian affairs in exchange for the release of the hostages. On January 20, 1981, the same day that Carter's successor, Ronald Reagan, was sworn in as president, the hostages were flown to Europe on their way back to America.

America's inability to rescue the hostages signaled to many at home and abroad that the United States had grown too inept and powerless to protect its citizens. It also signaled that the Soviets were winning the Cold War.

Chapter Six

Taking on the Evil Empire

"Let us be aware that while they preach the supremacy of the state, declare its omnipotence over individual man, and predict its eventual domination of all peoples on the Earth, they are the focus of evil in the modern world."

—Ronald Reagan describing the Soviet Union, March 8, 1983

The Soviet Union seemed to be at a high point in 1980. Communism was spreading in countries around the world, the USSR held a decisive advantage over America's nuclear and military forces, and the United States appeared to be in retreat in foreign affairs. The loss in Vietnam and the humiliation of the Iran hostage crisis led many American politicians and citizens to believe that the country's days as a world leader were over.

Ronald Reagan thought differently. A former Hollywood actor turned politician, Reagan became a hero to conservative Republicans for his plain-talking style and his patriotic sensibilities. Reagan served two terms as governor of California and was considered a contender for the White House in 1968 and 1976. By 1980 he had risen to the top of the Republican field, and he openly challenged Carter for his apparent lack of direction as president.

Reagan was a staunch anti-Communist who did not accept the popular view that America needed to share the world with the Soviet Union. When asked about his strategy for dealing with the Soviets, he responded, "We win, they lose."[55] His critics berated him for this simple view, but the American people handed him a resounding victory over Carter in the election.

Reagan embarked on a diplomatic course that differed greatly from his predecessor. His speeches attacked the Soviet Union as a soulless dictatorship that was a threat to world peace, and his policies openly challenged not just the USSR's place in international affairs but also its very right to exist.

America's Military Buildup

Reagan's strategy was summed up by Jack F. Matlock Jr., a member of the national security team during his presidency, "Deter further aggressive behavior by the Soviet Union, to make sure the Soviet leaders could never have the illusion that they could win a war with the United States, and . . . prepare the United States for successful negotiations."[56]

The first step in executing this strategy was to build up the American military. Carter had reluctantly reversed the nearly decade-old trend of paring down defense spending with the 1980 budget, but Reagan actively increased the size and quality of the American military. He wanted to achieve strategic superiority over the Soviets rather than parity. Defense spending rose from $171 billion to

An artist's rendering depicts a rocket-propelled missile racing to intercept a nuclear-tipped ballistic missile in flight high above the earth to prevent it from reaching its target. The American plan to extend its military reach against the Soviets into space, proposed by President Ronald Reagan in 1983, was formally called the Strategic Defense Initiative (SDI), but critics referred to it as "Star Wars."

$376 billion between 1981 and 1986, but it was not just greater numbers that America was pursuing during this time.

American military technology made a significant leap during the 1980s with new weapons systems reliant on advances in computer and satellite technology. Missile targeting became more precise than ever thought possible with multiple-targeted independent reentry vehicles, nuclear missiles that each contained several warheads that could strike different targets and be accurate within a few square yards.

Advances in laser technology allowed soldiers to hit targets with conventional weapons with startling accuracy. Satellite linkups and new computer systems allowed for better troop communications in the field. A program to develop bomber planes that were invisible to radar moved forward. The Navy went from 454 ships to 600. America also began researching a new missile defense program known as the Strategic Defense Initiative (SDI).

SDI was perhaps the most ambitious scientific and military program ever devised. It called for the creation of a vast network of satellite-based and land-based antiballistic missile platforms to track and destroy Soviet nuclear missiles in flight. Reagan first proposed the plan in a national television address on March 23, 1983. "I know this is a formidable, technical task, one that may not be accomplished before the end of this century. But isn't it worth every investment necessary to free the world from the threat of nuclear war? We know it is."[57]

SDI became a subject of widespread controversy. Some critics believed it was impossible to build and referred to it sarcastically as "Star Wars," implying that it was no more realistic than the science-fiction movie of the same name. Other scientists recognized that the technology was feasible, but it was enormously expensive, with cost estimates ranging as high as $1 trillion. The Soviets were convinced that America had the technology to build SDI, and it only enhanced their fears that Reagan was committed to building a nuclear arsenal to wipe out the USSR.

All opponents united behind the argument that SDI would actually destabilize the balance that existed between American and Soviet nuclear forces. Mutual assured destruction (MAD) ensured that a nuclear war would not break out between the superpowers because it meant universal destruction. SDI removed that balance because it would make it possible for America to destroy the Soviet Union in a nuclear strike while avoiding any significant damage in a Soviet counterstrike.

Reagan referred to MAD as "the craziest thing I ever heard of."[58] He believed that international stability should not come at the price of deliberately leaving the country open to nuclear attack. This rejection of a long-standing doctrine of deterrence caused unrest in the arms control community. Many politicians in the United States and among America's allies believed that Reagan's policies were making war between the superpowers more likely. The Soviets publicly embraced this

The Peacekeeper

The LGM-118A Peacekeeper, also known as the MX (missile experimental), was a nuclear missile that had been under development since the 1970s and was deployed beginning in 1986. Former Defense Department analyst Dennis Menos explains the role and power of the Peacekeeper:

A weapon of frightening size and lethal power, accurate enough to land its ten [300 kiloton] warheads within 300 feet [91m] of their targets. The mission of the MX in a first strike would be to destroy Soviet hardened missile silos and communication facilities and thus prevent retaliation. In theory, the MX could also be used in other missions, for example, in a counterforce role or to retaliate after a Soviet nuclear attack.

The MX was more lethal and more accurate than any missile that was deployed by the Soviets at the time, thus earning it the name Peacekeeper. It was considered a significant deterrent to Soviet aggression.

Although one hundred were originally commissioned, only fifty Peacekeepers were ever deployed. It was scheduled for elimination under the START II nuclear reduction agreement, and, although the agreement was never enforced, the last Peacekeeper was deactivated and scrapped in 2005.

Dennis Menos, *The Superpowers and Nuclear Arms Control.* New York: Praeger, 1990, p. 8.

A Peacekeeper missile, a highly accurate and destructive first-strike weapon designed to deter Soviet aggression, takes flight after a test launch at California's Vandenberg Air Force Base in May 1986.

view as well. Yuri Andropov, who became leader of the USSR after Brezhnev's death in 1982, said, "It is time they stopped devising one option after another in the search for the best ways of unleashing nuclear war in the hope of winning it."[59]

Unrest in the Communist Bloc

Years of rampant military spending at the expense of badly needed domestic services and the inherent failings of a state-planned economy were beginning to take their toll on the Soviet Union. Lack of access to adequate health care led to a declining life expectancy that was rare in industrialized nations. Lines stretched for blocks for basic items like bread and milk.

On paper, the Soviet Union had a successful economy in comparison to the United States. Between 1961 and 1984, for example, the USSR produced 80 percent more steel, 42 percent more oil, and twice as much pig iron as America. However, as Martin Walker points out, these statistics were misleading. "Had the world and its technologies stood still, the Soviet Union would have been an economic giant. . . . The West was living in an entirely different economic system, a post-industrial world in which the new sinews of wealth were microchips rather than pig-iron, plastic rather than steel."[60]

The inability of the state to provide basic needs was no longer being quietly tolerated by the new generation of citizens coming of age in the Communist bloc.

Lech Walesa, leader of striking workers in Poland, takes the podium to address a crowd outside of the Lenin Shipyard in Gdansk in August 1980.

These younger people yearned for the freedoms and services that were common in the West, and since they were too young to remember the terrors of Stalin, they did not fear punishment for speaking out. The threat of force was no longer a credible deterrent to prevent protests and unrest.

In July 1980 the Polish government mandated a steep increase in food prices. Workers across the country went on strike in protest. Led by Lech Walesa, an unemployed electrician, workers demanded and received the right to create the Solidarity trade union. Solidarity pushed for economic and political change in Poland. Prime Minister Wojciech Jaruzelski cracked down on the Solidarity union at the urging of Moscow, and thousands, including Walesa, were jailed.

Poland's handling of the Solidarity uprising drew widespread criticism from America and Western Europe. Reagan blamed the Soviets directly for repression in Poland, expressing publicly what many already believed—the Polish government, like all Communist governments in Eastern Europe, took their orders from Moscow. He ordered money and technical assistance to the Solidarity movement so that it could continue to function.

War in Central America

America also provided assistance to anti-Communist forces in Central America, but the growing level of involvement that Reagan insisted upon stirred controversy. In November 1981 the Central Intelligence Agency (CIA) was given funds to arm and train rebels committed to overthrowing the Sandinistas, a Communist dictatorship that toppled an America-friendly regime in Nicaragua in 1979.

The Contras, as the anti-Communist rebel group sworn to overthrow the Sandinistas came to be known, grew from a few hundred to fifteen thousand by the mid-1980s. CIA pilots flew in weapons and supplies, and American military advisers trained the Contras to execute raids against the Sandinistas from camps in nearby Honduras.

The United States also supported the government of El Salvador in its fight against Communist guerrillas that were supported by Cuba. Reagan increased aid from $36 million in 1981 to $197 million in 1984. The Salvadoran government's military leadership sent troops through the countryside and killed thousands of people, making no distinction between the guerrillas or the people who supported them. Their actions drew widespread international condemnation.

Reagan referred to the anti-Communists in El Salvador and Nicaragua as freedom fighters and appealed to the public and to Congress to support their cause. He noted in a May 9, 1984, speech, "This Communist subversion poses the threat that a hundred million people from Panama to the open border of our South could come under the control of pro-Soviet regimes."[61]

Public and political reaction to Reagan's call for support was mixed. Congress agreed to continue providing aid to the government of El Salvador, but

The Downing of
Flight KAL 007

On August 31, 1983, amidst tense relations between the United States and the Soviet Union, a Russian fighter plane shot down a Korean Air Lines jet that drifted off course into Soviet airspace. All 269 people on the plane were killed. The Soviets claimed that the plane, which strayed 365 miles (587km) off course, did not respond to repeated calls to change course. The fighter pilot identified the plane as a Boeing 747 commercial jet, yet he was still ordered to shoot it down. Authors Jeremy Isaacs and Taylor Downing write:

The response in Washington . . . was instant outrage. Secretary of State George Shultz said he could see "no explanation whatever for shooting down an unarmed commercial airliner, no matter whether it's in your airspace or not." Reagan expressed "revulsion at this horrifying act of violence." He called it a "terrorist act," "a crime against humanity," and "an act of barbarism." At the United Nations the U.S. representative described the shooting down of the civilian airliner as "wanton, calculated, deliberate murder." These furious condemnations were met with silence and evasions.

   The Soviets accused America of probing their air defenses with the jet, a charge that bore no merit and only caused greater tension between the superpowers.

Jeremy Isaacs and Taylor Downing, *Cold War: An Illustrated History, 1945–1991.* New York: Little, Brown, 1998, p. 346.

Reagan's approval of the mining of Nicaraguan ports and harbors angered many elected officials. They rejected sending more money or military support to the Contras, fearing an escalation of American involvement. A series of congressional actions collectively known as the Boland Amendments prohibited military funding, training, or support for the Contras. Reagan told National Security adviser Robert McFarlane, "I want to do whatever you have to do to help these people. . . . Do everything you can."[62]

   A complex plan was devised to raise money for the Contras through a series of illegal arms sales to Iran. Several members of Reagan's administration were involved, including McFarlane; his successor, Vice Admiral John Poindexter; and National Security Council staff associate lieutenant colonel Oliver North, who was in charge of the operational details.

   The operation, which became known as the Iran-Contra affair, was revealed in late 1986, and a Justice Department investigation led to convictions against Poindexter and North that were overturned on appeal. Reagan apologized to the nation during a nationally televised address on

March 4, 1987, and admitted ultimate responsibility for the actions of his subordinates even though he believed he did not know exactly what had taken place.

Reagan was willing to resort to direct intervention in stopping the spread of communism when he saw it necessary. A military coup in Grenada in October 1983 led to the deployment of U.S. forces for the first time since Vietnam to restore order on the tiny Caribbean island. Reagan believed that Grenada was meant to be a staging area for Cuban and Soviet military forces in the Caribbean and pointed to the construction of an airport there as an example. He was also concerned for the safety of several American medical students on the island. U.S. reaction was overwhelmingly positive, but international reaction was mostly hostile, with even America's allies accusing the country of interfering in the affairs of sovereign nations.

Nuclear Fears

The rapid expansion of the American military and its use in Grenada had Soviet leaders concerned over America's intentions,

German citizens form a human chain in the town of Amstetten in October 1983 to protest the deployment of U.S. missiles in Western Europe.

but the deployment of intermediate-range nuclear missiles in Europe convinced them that the United States was going to start a war. Pershing II missiles and 572 cruise missiles, capable of reaching Moscow from West German, Italian, and British bases in a matter of minutes, were added to the North Atlantic Treaty Organization arsenal in late 1983. The Soviets publicly stated that America was escalating tensions in Europe despite the fact that the Communist bloc possessed an equally deadly nuclear arsenal and a greater conventional military presence.

Many Western European citizens were openly hostile to the deployment of American missiles, and several countries refused to allow the weapons to be transported through their territory. Despite the failure of American détente in the 1970s, several Western European leaders still believed it was possible to achieve peace by accommodating the Soviet Union with unilateral disarmament. They also did not want to disrupt potential business opportunities with the Communist bloc.

Some American citizens also protested the country's military buildup, and critics of Reagan's policies called for a freeze on the production, testing, and deployment of nuclear weapons. They accused him of pursuing a policy that would only lead to a nuclear holocaust.

Fear of nuclear war was very much in the public mind, as the media of the time indicates. *The Fate of the Earth*, by Jonathan Schell, describes the devastating effects of nuclear war and became a best seller. The film *The Day After*, which graphically depicts the impact of a nuclear attack on a Midwestern town, drew one of the largest audiences in television history.

Reagan argued that his strategy to build up American forces would bring greater stability in U.S.–Soviet relations. In a speech Reagan gave in 1982, he said, "A Soviet leadership devoted to improving its people's lives, rather than expanding its armed conquests, will find a sympathetic partner in the West."[63]

Political Changes in Moscow

The Soviets experienced several changes in leadership during the mid-1980s. After Brezhnev's death on November 10, 1982, Yuri Andropov, the former leader of the KGB, the Soviet intelligence agency, became leader of the USSR. Andropov died on February 9, 1984, and the country was placed in the hands of Konstantin Chernenko, a seventy-two-year-old former staffer to Brezhnev who was so feeble that he had trouble delivering Andropov's eulogy.

The Kremlin was concerned that it chose leaders committed to communism in the spirit of the USSR's founders, which meant men born during the time of the 1917 Russian Revolution, but the old guard was dying out. When Chernenko died on March 19, 1985, the leadership was turned over to someone born after the 1917 revolution for the first time.

Mikhail Gorbachev was fifty-four years old when he became the head of the Soviet Union, and his age and his

Charlie Wilson's War

There was fierce American debate over how to combat the Soviets in Afghanistan during the early 1980s. The CIA was running support operations out of neighboring Pakistan, but Texas congressman Charles Wilson, a member of the House Appropriations Subcommittee on Defense, felt more needed to be done. He took it upon himself to get funding for the Mujahedeen, the Afghan rebels fighting the Soviets. Historian John Prados explains:

Democratic Congressman Charles Wilson of Texas waged what amounted to his own covert campaign against officials he thought insufficiently committed to the cause. . . . By dint of repeated travel to Pakistan, Wilson forged his own links to top Pakistani leaders. . . . He used these to encourage the Pakistanis to demand more than the CIA had programmed—more weapons and better ones too.

Reagan doubled what Carter had spent on Afghanistan. Congress, if anything, stayed ahead of the White House on the Afghan program. The CIA would ask for a couple of million dollars, Congress would appropriate twenty-five. Charlie Wilson became a sparkplug in this effort. The numbers only grew larger. In 1983 $30 million in CIA money ballooned with an extra $40 million in reprogrammed Pentagon funds demanded by Representative Wilson.

Wilson's commitment to supporting the Afghans in their fight against the Soviets helped contribute to the USSR's withdrawal from Afghanistan in 1989. Wilson retired from Congress in 1997.

John Prados, *Safe for Democracy: The Secret Wars of the CIA.* Chicago: Ivan R. Dee, 2006, p. 480.

---

ideas turned the nation in a direction no one ever thought possible. Gorbachev recognized a sincere need to reform the country soon or risk collapse. He noted, "Profound transformation must be carried out in the economy and the entire system of social relations, and a qualitatively higher standard of living must be ensured for the Soviet people."[64] Two new Russian words entered the Cold War vocabulary when Gorbachev emerged onto the scene: *perestroika*, meaning "reconstruction," and *glasnost*, meaning "openness."

Gorbachev's proposals represented a change that intrigued the United States, but old habits of secrecy were hard to break in the Soviet Union. On April 26, 1986, a reactor exploded at the Chernobyl nuclear power plant north of Kiev, Ukraine. Dozens were killed and hundreds hospitalized with radiation poisoning. Traditional Soviet secrecy and modern Soviet bureaucratic incompetence made for a deadly combination as a delayed evacuation and cleanup of the area caused several more deaths.

The disaster only became known to the world when monitoring stations in Europe detected the cloud of radioactive debris moving west. The Chernobyl accident and the poor manner in which the matter was handled was a great embarrassment to the Soviets and came to symbolize their crumbling system.

The Cold War Thaws in Europe

Relations between Reagan and Gorbachev started out tense when the two first met in Geneva, Switzerland, on November 19, 1985, but it soon became apparent that they had a mutual desire to rid the world of nuclear weapons. In fact, it seemed that Gorbachev was more willing to achieve total nuclear disarmament than Reagan when he proposed in January 1986 to pursue a nuclear-free world by 2000. Several members of Reagan's team did not take the proposal seriously, but Reagan himself was intrigued. He had originally proposed the elimination of all intermediate-range nuclear missiles from Europe in 1981, but the Soviets rejected the idea at the time.

Reagan and Gorbachev met in Reykjavik, Iceland, on October 11, 1986, in an attempt to make some headway on nuclear disarmament and humanitarian issues. The pace of the meeting shocked and delighted everyone concerned when the two leaders came within a handshake of eliminating all nuclear weapons within ten years. Gorbachev then demanded severe restrictions on SDI research, and it all fell apart. Reagan offered to share the technology with the Soviets once it had been perfected, but he absolutely refused to give up the program or confine research to the laboratory. Reagan equated the possession of the SDI to the fact that, "nations that pledged not to use poison gas didn't object if other nations had gas masks."[65]

Briefly after the Reykjavik meeting, it seemed that the United States and the Soviet Union would return to their traditional Cold War postures of mistrust and accusations. In February 1987, however, Gorbachev agreed to the elimination of U.S. and Soviet intermediate-range nuclear forces (INF) in Europe without the precondition of America abandoning the SDI.

President Ronald Reagan, left, and Soviet leader Mikhail Gorbachev meet in Reykjavik, Iceland, in October 1986 to discuss nuclear disarmament and humanitarian issues.

President Ronald Reagan implored Soviet leader Mikhail Gorbachev to "tear down this wall" in his famous speech delivered at the Brandenburg Gate in West Berlin in June 1987.

Reagan took this as a sign that the Soviets were starting to cave under years of U.S. pressure. On a trip to West Berlin, he took an opportunity to lay another challenge before the USSR in a June 12 speech at the Berlin Wall. "If you seek peace, if you seek prosperity for the Soviet Union and Eastern Europe, if you seek liberalization . . . Mr. Gorbachev, open this gate! Mr. Gorbachev, tear down this wall!"[66]

Gorbachev and Reagan met in Washington on December 8 and signed the INF Treaty. This historic agreement led to the complete dismantling of all U.S. and Soviet intermediate- and short-range nuclear weapons in Europe. For the next two days, Gorbachev stayed in Washington, where he was met by enthusiastic crowds and well-wishers. Reagan received a similar greeting in Moscow in May 1988. It became clear that not only were the American and Soviet leaders no longer enemies, but they had actually become friends.

Chapter Seven

The Fall of the Soviet Union

"A standard Soviet-era joke was that capitalism was the exploitation of man by man, whereas communism was the reverse."

—Norman Friedman, *The Fifty-Year War: Conflict and Strategy in the Cold War*

Ronald Reagan left office in January 1989 with relations between the United States and the USSR fundamentally changed. The tense standoff between the superpowers that held the world at the brink of nuclear war for decades had eased to a level of calm never before experienced. Reagan's successor, George H.W. Bush, wanted to continue moving toward a peaceful coexistence with the Soviets, but he wanted to proceed cautiously.

Unlike Reagan or Carter when they entered the White House, Bush had a lengthy résumé in foreign policy. He served as America's ambassador to the United Nations under Richard Nixon, as the head of the Central Intelligence Agency under Gerald Ford, and as vice president under Reagan. He believed there were momentous opportunities to be gained in working with the Soviets, but he also believed that there was still the possibility that things could go wrong. Economic troubles had multiplied in the Soviet Union, and glasnost inspired the Russian people to begin publicly speaking out against their government.

Mikhail Gorbachev was impatient to move forward. In December 1988, after Bush won the election, he urged the president-elect to move forward with the same spirit as Reagan. "I'm doing this because there's a revolution taking place in my country," Gorbachev said. "I started it. And they all applauded me when I started it in 1986, and now they don't like it so much."[67]

The Communist Bloc Disintegrates

Opposition to Gorbachev became apparent in the Kremlin after the Intermediate-Range Nuclear Forces Treaty was signed, and many were blaming his policies for the economic turbulence Russia was experiencing. Inflation and unemployment combined with a shortage of industrial and commercial goods to make the Soviet Union appear as if it were a third-world country.

Gorbachev was not willing to stop. He believed that the only way to get Russia's economy under control was to relieve the massive burden of military spending, which accounted for 50 percent of the gross domestic product. In a speech before the UN General Assembly on December 7, 1988, Gorbachev announced unilateral cuts of five hundred thousand soldiers, ten thousand tanks, eighty-five hundred artillery pieces, and eight hundred combat aircraft from Eastern Europe. Similarly, deep cuts were being made along the Chinese border in the east.

The signal had gone out that the Communist states of the Warsaw Pact were on their own. The Soviets would no longer interfere to prop up their regimes like they had in Hungary in 1956 and in Czechoslovakia in 1968. The leaders of unpopular regimes in Poland, East Germany, Romania, and elsewhere now had to face their citizens.

The Polish parliament voted to allow multiparty elections, and in June the Solidarity Party won ninety-nine of one

East German guards atop the Berlin Wall watch as crowds wave the German flag in celebration of the November 1989 opening of the border checkpoints that divided east from west in the city for nearly thirty years.

The Massacre in Tianmen Square

Beginning on April 15, 1989, as many as 1 million Chinese students, labor activists, and intellectuals took to the streets of Beijing calling for democratic reforms. Debate raged in the government about how to handle the peaceful demonstrations. Chinese officials soon began to fear that the demonstrations could lead to a toppling of the government. On June 3 the Chinese government ordered the following actions:

Army units supported by tanks were sent in to clear the streets of demonstrators. In the massacre that followed, an unknown number of young Chinese were killed, their bodies rapidly gathered before they could be counted. All estimates suggested that the number of dead ran into hundreds. The massacre took place in full view of the world's media . . . immensely discrediting the Chinese leadership. After the bloodbath, thousands more were arrested and imprisoned. The Democracy Movement in China was finished for many years.

Ironically, the Tiananmen Square massacre had a positive effect on events in Eastern Europe later in 1989. It showed that force was no longer an option against large-scale public demonstrations. In a world of instant global communications, no European government gunning down opponents could maintain credibility and survive.

Jeremy Isaacs and Taylor Downing, *Cold War: An Illustrated History, 1945–1991.* New York: Little, Brown, 1998, p. 380.

Chinese protesters march under a poster of Communist leader Mao Zedong in Beijing's Tiananmen Square in the spring of 1989, demanding the government enact democratic reforms.

hundred seats in the senate and a majority of open seats in the lower house. Hungary also voted to allow open elections. It opened its border with Austria, and found East German refugees crossing through Czechoslovakia into Hungary to escape to Austria and the West. On September 10, ignoring the protests of East German leader Erich Honecker, the Hungarian government freely allowed East Germans to use its country as a gateway out of the Communist bloc. Within three days thirteen thousand East German citizens fled to the West.

Honecker, a hard-liner who had led East Germany for eighteen years, was determined to maintain order. He sealed the East German border with Czechoslovakia. As large crowds of protesers gathered in the streets of East Berlin and Leipzig, Gorbachev made a personal appeal to Honecker to enact reforms. Honecker refused and ordered his troops to open fire on the protesters. The troops refused, and Honecker was removed from office in a coup.

In an attempt to relieve the pressure of the demonstrations, the new leaders of East Germany agreed to issue visas to those wishing to visit the West. On November 9, 1989, thousands of East German citizens gathered at the checkpoints of the Berlin Wall. Flustered border guards gave in to the will of the crowd to open the gates, and East and West Berliners rushed through the checkpoints to greet one another. Bold Germans armed with hammers and chisels began breaking down the wall. Within a year, the concrete barricade that had divided

Berlin for twenty-eight years was gone.

The fall of communism in Eastern Europe had been remarkably peaceful, with the exception of events in Romania in December 1989. Stalinist leader Nicolae Ceausescu had ruled Romania with an iron hand since 1965, but his days were numbered when security troops shot several demonstrators in Transylvania. On December 23 Ceausescu and his wife, Elena, fled as the army transferred allegiance to a new government. They were promptly caught, put on trial, and executed on December 25, 1989.

The Communist bloc in Eastern Europe was finished.

Malta

Bush received a great deal of criticism for sitting on the sidelines while history was being made in Europe. A policy review of U.S.–Soviet relations that his administration was creating took months to deliver, and political supporters in America and Gorbachev himself began to lose faith in the American president's ability to act. Bush was aware of the image that was being portrayed and grew frustrated over the lack of progress in developing a renewed disarmament strategy. He angrily told his staff, "Don't keep telling me why it can't be done. Tell me how it can be done."[68]

Bush and Gorbachev met off the coast of Malta on December 2 and 3 to discuss further disarmament. They agreed to move forward with a Strategic Arms Reduction Treaty (START), which would lead to a further reduction in nuclear weapons. There were also plans to reduce

President George H.W. Bush, left, and Soviet leader Mikhail Gorbachev discuss the development of the Strategic Arms Reduction Treaty (START) at their summit meeting in Malta in December 1989.

chemical weapons stockpiles and conventional forces. The Soviets had already begun their withdrawal from Afghanistan, and they agreed to halt arms shipments to Central America.

One of the most significant pledges Gorbachev received from Bush was the promise to move beyond containment and offer economic support to the Soviet Union. Bush offered to normalize trade relations and support the USSR's entry into the General Agreement on Tariffs and Trade. Gorbachev agreed to turn the Soviet economy "sharply toward cooperation with other countries, so that it would be part and parcel of the world economic system."[69]

Turmoil in Russia

Gorbachev was bombarded with demands for independence when he traveled to Lithuania in early January 1990.

The Baltic states of Lithuania, Latvia, and Estonia had been annexed by Stalin in 1939 and were eager to break away from the Soviet Union. Gorbachev refused because he knew other republics would follow.

Upon his return to Moscow, Gorbachev confronted a crisis in the Soviet republic of Azerbaijan when ethnic rioting broke out. Troops were dispatched, and several hundred demonstrators were killed. Demonstrations erupted in Moscow and several other cities across the Soviet Union with citizens demanding more electoral freedom.

On February 5 Gorbachev told the Soviet Central Committee, "The Party will be able to fulfill its mission . . . only if it drastically restructures itself . . . and cooperates with all forces committed to perestroika."[70] The Soviet constitution was changed to allow more political parties to run for office, and a new office of the president was created so that Gorbachev would have more power to enact his reforms.

Despite these dramatic constitutional changes, prices continued to rise and the economy continued to sink. Gorbachev was rapidly losing support for his programs. On May 29 Boris Yeltsin was chosen leader of the Russian Republic. Yeltsin had resigned from the Communist Party and was opposed to Gorbachev's manipulation of the constitution. Upon his election, the Russian parliament announced that its laws took precedence over Soviet laws. Between July and October, Ukraine and five other republics also declared their sovereignty.

The Soviet Union passed laws guaranteeing freedom of worship and removing the media from state control, but it still was not enough. Gorbachev attempted throughout the first half of 1991 to shore up American economic support, but the more desperate the situation became, the more reluctant the United States was to offer aid.

On August 19, 1991, while Gorbachev was on holiday in the Black Sea, a state of emergency was announced on radio and television across the USSR. The country was told that Gorbachev was ill and presidential powers had been transferred to Vice President Gennady Yanayev. In reality, a coup was under

Russian president Boris Yeltsin, left, stands with supporters atop a tank at the Russian parliament building after a failed August 1991 coup attempt to oust Soviet leader Mikhail Gorbachev in the wake of demands for independence from a number of Soviet republics.

way. Several members of the government confronted Gorbachev and demanded that he sign over emergency powers to Yanayev. He refused and was placed under house arrest.

Yeltsin denounced the coup, and thousands of supporters joined him at the Russian parliament building. The plotters, led by Yanayev, either did not have the nerve or the knowledge necessary to follow through with what they had started. Within a matter of days, the coup was finished and Gorbachev returned to Moscow.

The Soviet Union Dissolves

The plot to overthrow Gorbachev had failed, but the courage that Yeltsin demonstrated during the coup left him the master of Russia's destiny. Gorbachev resigned as leader of the Communist Party on August 24, and the Communist Party itself disbanded on August 29. Yeltsin and the leaders of Ukraine and Belarus signed an agreement on December 8 that ended the USSR and created the Commonwealth of Independent States. Eight other former Soviet republics joined the commonwealth on December 21.

On December 25 only one last act remained for the president of the USSR. In a televised address, Gorbachev announced, "I hereby discontinue my activities in the post of president of the Union of Soviet Socialist Republics."[71] Later that day the red hammer-and-sickle flag of the Soviet Union, which had flown over the Kremlin for seventy years, was lowered for the last time.

The Aftermath

Boris Yeltsin's rule over Russia began with promise, but his government became plagued by corruption and serious economic difficulties. A ruling class of oligarchs, politicians, and businessmen who gained great wealth after the fall of communism ran the country. The military was scaled back, and the nuclear weapons that existed in other republics were transferred to Russia, which agreed to abide by the START agreement that had been signed by Gorbachev.

World events moved on without Russia playing a central role. East and West Germany were reunited as one nation in 1990, and several former Communist countries joined the European Union and applied for membership in the North Atlantic Treaty Organization. Ethnic tensions in former Soviet states flared up in the 1990s, due in large part to a lack of leadership from Moscow, which kept such issues under control for decades. Genocide in Yugoslavia and civil war in Chechnya, a Russian republic, remained troubling issues throughout the decade.

The United States settled into its role as the world's sole superpower, accepting a level of responsibility in foreign affairs rivaled in history only by the British and Roman empires. America's military dominance was on full display in the Persian Gulf War of 1991, in which it forcibly ejected Iraq from the oil-rich nation of Kuwait. America scaled back its military spending somewhat in the 1990s from Cold War levels. That trend was reversed after the terrorist attacks of September

The Mitrokhin Archive

Vasili Mitrokhin was a senior archivist for the KGB who had grown disillusioned with his government during the Cold War. His job allowed him access to numerous documents that demonstrated the systematic repression of the Russian people at the hands of the KGB. In 1972 he was put in charge of moving the archive of the first chief directorate from Lubyanka to Yasenevo.

While supervising the checking of files, the compilation of inventories and the writing of index cards, Mitrokhin was able to inspect what files he wished in one or the other of his offices. Few KGB officers apart from Mitrokhin have ever spent as much time reading, let alone noting, foreign intelligence files. . . .

Each night when he returned to his Moscow flat, Mitrokhin hid his notes beneath his mattress. On weekends he took them to a family dacha [vacation home] thirty-six kilometers [22 miles] from Moscow and typed up as many as possible. . . . He hid the first batches of typescripts and notes in a milk-churn which he buried below the floor. . . . When the milk-churn was full, he began concealing his notes and typescripts in a tin clothes-boiler. Eventually, his archive also filled two tin trunks and two aluminum cases, all of them buried beneath the dacha.

The Mitrokhin Archive, as the treasure of documents came to be known, was secretly transported to England after Mitrokhin told British intelligence of its existence in 1992. The archive is the single largest collection of Soviet-era documents to escape Russia after the Cold War and details a great extent of the secret operations undertaken by the Soviets to undermine the West.

Christopher Andrew and Vasili Mitrokhin, *The Sword and the Shield: The Mitrokhin Archive and the Secret History of the KGB.* New York: Basic Books, 1999, pp. 8, 10.

11, 2001, and the United States currently maintains an annual defense budget in excess of $500 billion, far exceeding that of any other nation, including China, which has committed to a major military buildup that some experts believe will put China on par with the United States in the next fifteen to twenty years.

Although the United States remains the world's single most powerful nation and the Communist threat has disappeared, the world is not at peace. Radical Islamic fundamentalism has become the single largest threat to stability in international affairs. Between 1993 and 2001 the United States and its allies were the targets of several terrorist attacks meant to force America to withdraw from involvement in the Middle East. The fundamentalists seek to create a Muslim state that would control that region of the world and its energy resources, as well as

Vladimir Putin: Father of a New Russia

Vladimir Putin is technically not the most powerful man in Russia; that distinction belongs to President Dmitri Medvedev. But Putin was president from 2000 until 2008, and it was his heavy-handed support that put Medvedev in office, an act that was promptly rewarded with an appointment as prime minister. Reporter Adi Ignatius writes about Putin's role in Russia and the world:

[P]utin] has restored stability and a sense of pride among citizens who, after years of Soviet stagnation, rode the heartbreaking roller coaster of raised and dashed expectations when Gorbachev and then Yeltsin were in charge. A basket case in the 1990s, Russia's economy has grown an average of 7 percent a year for the past five years. The country has paid off a foreign debt that once neared $200 billion. Russia's rich have gotten rich, often obscenely so.

But all this has a dark side. To achieve stability, Putin and his administration have dramatically curtailed freedoms. His government has shut down TV stations and newspapers, jailed businessmen whose wealth and influence challenged the Kremlin's hold on power, defanged opposition political parties and arrested those who confronted his rule.

Putin remains popular in Russia despite his undemocratic ways. He has also demonstrated a willingness to oppose the United States on a number of complex international issues, including holding North Korea and Iran to account for their pursuit of nuclear weapons. Although the Cold War is over, the challenges of stable relations between East and West remain.

Adi Ignatius, "A Tsar Is Born," *Time,* December 31, 2007, p. 49.

Vladimir Putin, who served as president of Russia from 2000 to 2008, is credited with rebuilding the Russian economy while also adopting many undemocratic policies to deal with what he perceived to be threats to his power.

subject its people to a tyrannical religious dictatorship.

Regions of the world that were once ideological or military battlegrounds over which the United States and the Soviets vied for supremacy are once again the scenes of war. Islamic fundamentalists in Afghanistan, once allied with the United States against the Soviet invasion, are being hunted by the U.S. military for their involvement in terrorist attacks that have claimed thousands of innocent lives in America, Europe, and elsewhere.

Another former Cold War ally, Iraq, became America's enemy after the Soviet Union dissolved. Dictator Saddam Hussein received American support in his battle for Middle Eastern supremacy against Soviet-backed Iran from 1980 until 1988. After the 1991 Persian Gulf War, America gathered evidence that Saddam was supporting terrorists seeking to attack Israel and the United States.

Believing that Saddam was supporting the very Islamic terrorists who were killing Americans, the United States invaded Iraq in March 2003 after Saddam refused to open up his country to a complete search for weapons of mass destruction. Saddam was removed from power, and the democratically elected government in Iraq that replaced the dictator put him on trial and executed him for the deaths of many thousands of Iraqi civilians who had opposed him during his rule. The United States remains engaged in a military campaign against Islamic fundamentalists in Iraq that has caused much political strife domestically.

Nuclear proliferation is also a major cause for concern. Iran, Syria, and North Korea remain committed to developing their own nuclear programs despite economic sanctions and the widespread condemnation of the international community. Weapons in the hands of such unstable tyrannical regimes would severely destabilize the Middle East and Asia, creating a new arms race that would threaten the lives of millions. Furthermore, it is possible that such weapons could be sold to the same terrorist groups that are currently waging war against the United States.

Very few people ever believed that the Cold War would end peacefully, yet it did. However, the end of the fifty-year conflict between the United States and the Soviet Union did not bring world peace. A whole series of unique challenges faced the victor, and now, a world once balanced equally between two foes is now reliant on the power of a single nation to bring order and prosperity to the world. Whether America is up to the challenge remains to be seen. It will need to draw upon the lessons learned in fighting the Cold War during the last half of the twentieth century, but it will also have to develop new strategies and new ideas to face the challenges posed in the twenty-first century. What will remain important in the future, as in the past, is America's commitment to freedom and democracy for itself and for all nations.

Notes

Introduction: One War Leads to Another

1. Quoted in Ronald E. Powaski, *The Cold War: The United States and the Soviet Union, 1917–1991*. New York: Oxford University Press, 1998, p. 47.
2. Quoted in Martin Walker, *The Cold War: A History*. New York: Henry Holt, 1993, p. 12.
3. Powaski, *The Cold War*, p. 64.
4. Quoted in Lisle A. Rose, *The Cold War Comes to Main Street*. Lawrence: University Press of Kansas, 1999, p. 24.

Chapter One: The Iron Curtain

5. Norman Friedman, *The Fifty-Year War: Conflict and Strategy in the Cold War*. Annapolis, MD: Naval Institute, 2000, p. 31.
6. Quoted in Walker, *The Cold War*, p. 28.
7. Friedman, *The Fifty-Year War*, p. 64.
8. Quoted in John Lewis Gaddis, *Strategies of Containment: A Critical Appraisal of American National Security Policy During the Cold War*. New York: Oxford University Press, 2005, p. 22.
9. George Kennan, "The Sources of Soviet Conduct," *Foreign Affairs*, July 1947. www.foreignaffairs.org/19470701faessay25403/x/the-sources-of-soviet-conduct.html.
10. United States Intelligence Community, "National Security Act of 1947," title I, sec. 103. www.intelligence.gov/0-natsecact_1947.shtml#s102a.
11. Quoted in Gaddis, *Strategies of Containment*, p. 39.
12. Quoted in "European Initiative Essential to Economic Recovery," *Department of State Bulletin*, June 15, 1947, p. 1160.
13. Walker, *The Cold War*, p. 49.
14. Friedman, *The Fifty-Year War*, p. 137.

Chapter Two: New Commitments, New Dangers

15. Walker, *The Cold War*, p. 62.
16. Dean Acheson, *Present at the Creation: My Years at the State Department*. New York: W.W. Norton, 1969, p. 355.
17. Quoted in Powaski, *The Cold War*, p. 82.
18. Walker, *The Cold War*, p. 74.
19. Quoted in William Manchester, *American Caesar*. New York: Random House, 1978, p. 722.
20. CNN.com, *Cold War*, "Episode 5: Korea." www.cnn.com/SPECIALS/cold.war/episodes/05/documents/macarthur.
21. Walker, *The Cold War*, p. 77.
22. Lisle A. Rose, *The Cold War Comes to Main Street: America in 1950*. Lawrence: University of Kansas Press, 1999, p. 115.
23. Quoted in Rose, *The Cold War Comes to Main Street*, p. 122.
24. Quoted in Stephen E. Ambrose, *Nixon: The Education of a Politician*,

1913–1962. New York: Simon & Schuster, 1987, p. 340.

Chapter Three: The Cold War Goes Global

25. Quoted in Dwight D. Eisenhower Presidential Library and Museum, "January 20, 1953, Inaugural Address." www.eisenhower.archives.gov/speeches/1953_inaugural_address.html.
26. Quoted in Gaddis, *Strategies of Containment*, p. 128.
27. Quoted in Walker, *The Cold War*, p. 96.
28. Quoted in Richard H. Immerman, *John Foster Dulles: Piety, Pragmatism, and Power in U.S. Foreign Policy*. Wilmington, DE: Scholarly Resources, 1999, p. 84.
29. John Lewis Gaddis, *We Now Know: Rethinking Cold War History*. Oxford, UK: Oxford University Press, 1997, p. 224.
30. Gaddis, *We Now Know*, p. 234.
31. Patrick Glynn, *Closing Pandora's Box: Arms Races, Arms Control, and the History of the Cold War*. New York: Basic-Books, 1992, p. 173.
32. Quoted in American Presidency Project, "Dwight D. Eisenhower: Address at the Annual Convention of the National Junior Chamber of Commerce, Minneapolis, Minnesota," June 10, 1953. www.presidency.ucsb.edu/ws/index.php?pid=9871&st=&st1=.
33. Quoted in John Prados, *Safe for Democracy: The Secret Wars of the CIA*. Chicago: Ivan R. Dee, 2006, p. 107.
34. Powaski, *The Cold War*, p. 121.
35. Jeremy Isaacs and Taylor Downing, *Cold War: An Illustrated History, 1945–1991*. New York: Little, Brown, 1998, p. 160.

Chapter Four: The Success and Failure of Flexible Response

36. Maxwell D. Taylor, *The Uncertain Trumpet*. New York: Harper & Brothers, 1960, p. 5.
37. Quoted in Friedman, *The Fifty-Year War*, p. 255.
38. Quoted in Isaacs and Downing, *Cold War*, p. 173.
39. Robert F. Kennedy, *Thirteen Days: A Memoir of the Cuban Missile Crisis*. New York: W.W. Norton, 1968, p. 28.
40. Quoted in Kennedy, *Thirteen Days*, p. 152.
41. Walker, *The Cold War*, p. 171.
42. Quoted in Powaski, *The Cold War*, p. 148.
43. Quoted in Barbara W. Tuchman, *The March of Folly*. New York: Alfred A. Knopf, 1984, p. 311.
44. Quoted in American Presidency Project, "Richard Nixon: Address Accepting the Presidential Nomination at the Republican National Convention in Miami Beach, Florida," August 8, 1968. www.presidency.ucsb.edu/ws/index.php?pid=25968.

Chapter Five: A New Approach

45. Henry Kissinger, *White House Years*. Boston: Little, Brown, 1979, p. 192.
46. Kissinger, *White House Years*, p. 272.
47. Quoted in Kissinger, *White House Years*, p. 164.
48. Quoted in Glynn, *Closing Pandora's Box*, p. 256.
49. Quoted in Gaddis, *Strategies of Containment*, p. 278.
50. Quoted in Glynn, *Closing Pandora's Box*, p. 271.

51. Gaddis, *Strategies of Containment*, p. 318.
52. Friedman, *The Fifty-Year War*, p. 386.
53. Quoted in Cold War International History Project, "CPSU CC Protocol #46/10," February 18, 1977. http://wilsoncenter.org/index.cfm?topic_id=1409&fuseaction=va2.document&identifier=5034F24D-96B6-175C-9109BF6E207A4117&sort=Collection&item=US-Soviet%20Relations.
54. Quoted in Glynn, *Closing Pandora's Box*, p. 304.

Chapter Six: Taking on the Evil Empire

55. Quoted in Richard Reeves, *President Reagan: Triumph of the Imagination*. New York: Simon & Schuster, 2005, p. 6.
56. Jack F. Matlock, Jr., *Reagan and Gorbachev: How the Cold War Ended*. New York: Random House, 2004, p. 6.
57. Quoted in Ronald Reagan Presidential Library, "Address to the Nation on Defense and National Security," March 23, 1983. www.reagan.utexas.edu/archives/speeches/1983/32383d.htm.
58. Ronald Reagan, *An American Life*. New York: Simon & Schuster, 1990, p. 13.
59. Quoted in Isaacs and Downing, *Cold War*, p. 342.
60. Walker, *The Cold War*, p. 234.
61. Quoted in Ronald Reagan Presidential Library, "Address to the Nation on United States Policy in Central America," May 9, 1984. www.reagan.utexas.edu/archives/speeches/1984/50984h.htm.
62. Quoted in Reeves, *President Reagan*, p. 221.
63. Quoted in Matlock, *Reagan and Gorbachev*, p. 3.
64. Quoted in Isaacs and Downing, *Cold War*, p. 355.
65. Quoted in Matlock, *Reagan and Gorbachev*, p. 234.
66. Quoted in Reeves, *President Reagan*, p. 401.

Chapter Seven: The Fall of the Soviet Union

67. Quoted in Michael R. Beschloss and Strobe Talbott, *At the Highest Levels: The Inside Story of the End of the Cold War*. Boston: Little, Brown, 1993, p. 11.
68. Quoted in Isaacs and Downing, *Cold War*, p. 378.
69. Quoted in Powaski, *The Cold War*, p. 270.
70. Quoted in Beschloss and Talbott, *At the Highest Levels*, p. 178.
71. Quoted in Beschloss and Talbott, *At the Highest Levels*, p. 463.

Glossary

armistice: A truce between two nations in conflict.

Communist bloc: The group of nations that were under Communist control during the Cold War.

containment: An American strategy to keep the Soviet Union from spreading communism beyond its borders.

coup: An overthrow of a government by a group within that nation, generally military officers or rebel groups.

dissent: Opposition to the government authority in the form of protests or other political action.

doctrine: A stated position or policy that becomes the standard of behavior for a government.

gross domestic product: The total value of the goods and services produced by a particular nation or group; the standard measurement for a nation's productivity.

ideology: The theories or ideas of a political group, nation, or even a group of nations that become the guiding characteristics for that group's cultural and political behavior.

insurgency: A rebellion within a country in which a particular group seeks power.

isolationist: A person or group position that wishes not to be engaged in international matters that it feels does not directly affect the safety and welfare of one's own country.

oligarch: A person who is a member of a national ruling elite that is unelected and unaccountable to the public.

satellite state: A nation that is closely allied to a larger country that has power over its actions; for example, East Germany was a satellite state of the Soviet Union.

subversive: Actions taken in an attempt to overthrow or cause the destruction of a government.

totalitarianism: A system of government in which absolute power is held by a highly centralized authority.

unilateral: An action taken by one party or one nation without being prompted by any other party or nation; not mutual.

For Further Exploration

Books

Walter L. Hixson, *Parting the Curtain: Propaganda, Culture, and the Cold War, 1945–1961.* Hampshire, UK: Palgrave Macmillan, 1997. This book examines America's psychological warfare programs directed against the Soviets during the Truman and Eisenhower presidencies.

Jeremy Isaacs and Taylor Downing, *Cold War: An Illustrated History, 1945–1991.* New York: Little, Brown, 1998. A richly illustrated text that is the companion piece to the CNN television series.

Edward H. Judge and John W. Langdon, *The Cold War: A History Through Documents.* New York: Prentice Hall, 1998. A collection of important speeches, treaties, and articles that shaped the Cold War.

Stephen Wagg and David L. Andrews, *East Plays West: Sport and the Cold War.* New York: Routledge, 2006. This work explores the nature of athletic competition between the superpowers during the Cold War and how it affected relations.

Stephen J. Whitfield, *The Culture of the Cold War: The American Moment.* Baltimore: Johns Hopkins University Press, 1996. This book explores the impact of the Cold War on America's national identity.

Internet Sources

Cold War (www.cnn.com/SPECIALS /cold.war). Based on the CNN television series, this site contains complete information about each episode and additional material on espionage, technology, and culture of the Cold War.

Cold War International History Project (http://wilsoncenter.org/index.cfm? fuseaction=topics.home&topic _id=1409). This site offers new information and perspectives on the history of the Cold War, in particular new findings from previously inaccessible sources on "the other side"—the former Communist world.

Cold War Museum (www.coldwar.org/ index.html). An online trivia and general information site about the Cold War, which includes a free subscription to a quarterly magazine, the *Cold War Times.*

Documents Related to American Foreign Policy: Cold War (www.mthol yoke.edu/acad/intrel/coldwar.htm). A comprehensive listing of thousands of speeches, cables, memoranda, and policy statements relating to the Cold War.

NASA History Division (http://history. nasa.gov). This Web site is devoted to the history of NASA and America's space program.

National Security Archive (www.gwu. edu/~nsarchiv). Sponsored by George Washington University, this site offers recently declassified information obtained through Freedom of Information requests to the U.S. government.

Presidential Libraries. Each president of the Cold War has an online library devoted to his administration that contains speeches, historical anecdotes, and photographs:

Harry S. Truman (www.trumanlibrary. org).

Dwight D. Eisenhower (www.eisenhower.archives.gov).

John F. Kennedy (www.jfklibrary.org).

Lyndon Johnson (http://lbjlib.utexas.edu).

Richard Nixon (http://Nixon.archives. gov).

Gerald Ford (www.fordlibrarymuseum. gov).

Jimmy Carter (www.jimmycarterlibrary. gov).

Ronald Reagan (www.reagan.utexas. edu).

George H.W. Bush (http://bushlibrary. tamu.edu).

Index

A

Acheson, Dean, 27, 34
Afghanistan, 70, 81, 93
Allende Gossens, Salvador, 62
Allies, 9–10
American culture, 45–48
Americans
    antiwar sentiment of, 59–60
    fear of nuclear war by, 45–48
Andropov, Yuri, 76, 80
Anglo-Iranian Oil Company,
    42–43
Angola, 66
Anti-Ballistic Missile (ABM)
    Treaty, 65–66
Antiwar protests, 59–60
Apollo-Soyuz Test Project
    (ASTP), 67
Arbenz Guzman, Jacobo,
    43–44
Arms control agreements
    ABM Treaty, 65–66
    INF Treaty, 83, 85
    SALT, 68
    SALT II, 70
    START, 87–88
Arms race. *See* Nuclear arms
    race
Army-McCarthy hearings, 35
Arnold, Hap, 20
Atmospheric Test Ban Treaty,
    54
Atomic bomb, 11, 23–24, 25
Atomic diplomacy, 17
Atomic spy ring, 33
Attlee, Clement, 10
Azerbaijan, 88

B

B-52 bomber, 41
Balance of power, 66
Ballistic missiles, 41, 57, 68
Baltics, 15, 88–89
Baruch, Bernard, 23
Bay of Pigs, 50, 52

Beisner, Robert L., 34
Berkeley, Martin, 36
Berlin
    division of, 10, 15
    Soviet blockage of, 20–21
Berlin Airlift, 20–21
Berlin Wall, 51, 52, 83, 87
Bessie, Alvah, 36
Biberman, Herbert, 36
Blacklisting, 36
Boland Amendments, 78
Brezhnev, Leonid, 57, 63, 65, 80
Brown, Harold, 70
Brzezinski, Zbigniew, 70
Bulgaria, 15
Burlatsky, Fyodor, 54
Bush, George H. W., 84, 87–88
Buster-Jangle test, 40

C

Cambodia, 66
Capitalism, 8, 32
Carter, Jimmy, 68, 70–71
Castro, Fidel, 50, 62
Ceausescu, Nicolae, 87
Censorship, 17
Central America, 43–44, 77–80
Central Intelligence Agency
    (CIA), 18, 43, 62, 77
Chambers, Whitaker, 33–34
Chechnya, 90
Chernenko, Konstantin, 80
Chernobyl disaster, 81–82
Chiang Kaishek, 26–27
Chile, 62
China
    Communist takeover of,
        25–27
    Korean War and, 30, 32
    military buildup in, 91
    relations between Soviets
        and, 63–65
    Tianmen Square massacre, 86
Churchill, Winston, 9–10, 15
Civil defense strategies, 47–48

Clay, Lucius, 20
Cold War
    defined, 23
    Europe during, 13
    ideological basis of, 8–9
    interventionism during,
        42–44
    thawing of, in Europe, 82–83
    U.S. worldview during, 38
Cole, Lester, 36
Communism
    in China, 25–27
    containment of, 17–18, 27–28,
        38
    fall of, 85, 87
    fear of, 45–48
    in Soviet Union, 8–9
    spread of, 12, 15, 17–18
    Truman's stance on, 27
    U.S. view of, 32–33
Communist bloc
    countries of, 12, 15, 17
    unrest in, 76–77
Communist Party, 8, 15, 90
Communist propaganda, 17
Communist
    sympathizers/spies, 33–34
Containment policy, 16–18,
    27–28, 38
Contras, 77, 78
Cooper-Church Amendment,
    63
Cowan, George, 40–41
Cuba, 49, 50
Cuban Missile Crisis, 52–54
Czechoslovakia, 21, 63, 85

D

The Day After (film), 80
Defense spending
    after 9/11, 90–91
    during Cold War, 18, 32, 38,
        68
    decreased, 68
    increase in, under Reagan,

73–74
in Soviet Union, 85
Department of Defense, 18
Détente, 63–66, 67, 68
Deterrence
MAD, 41–42, 74
through massive retaliation, 39, 41–42
Dissent, 17
Dissidents, 68
Dmytryk, Edward, 36
Dominican Republic, 58
Duck and cover drills, 46, 47
Dulles, John Foster, 38, 39

E
Eagle Claw, 71
East Germany, 85, 87
Eastern Europe
Communist takeover of, 15
under Communist control, 10, 12, 17
fall of communism in, 85, 87
Economic boom, post-WWII, 13
Einstein, Albert, 37
Eisenhower, Dwight D.
during Cold War, 41
defense policy of, 38–39
election of, 37
overseas commitments by, 44
on Soviets, 50
El Salvador, 77
Estonia, 15, 88
Europe
during Cold War, 13
missile buildup in, 80
postwar, 10
rebuilding of, post-WWII, 14–20
thawing of Cold War in, 82–83
See also Eastern Europe;
Western Europe
European Union, 90
Executive Committee, 53
Explorer 1, 45

F
Fallout shelters, 47
Fate of the Earth (Schell), 80
Federal Civil Defense
Administration, 47
Fleming, Ian, 46
Fleming, Thomas, 31
Flexible response doctrine,

49–50, 57
Ford, Gerald, 66
Forrestal, James, 18
Free-market capitalism, 8, 32
Friedman, Norman, 14, 17, 24, 68
Fuchs, Klaus, 23–24, 33

G
Gaddis, John Lewis, 41, 68
General Agreement on Tariffs
and Trade (GATT), 88
Germany
division of, 10, 15
East, 85, 87
postwar, 10, 15, 20
reunification of, 90
West, 21
Glasnost, 81, 84
Glynn, Patrick, 42
Gold, Harry, 33
Gorbachev, Mikhail
Bush and, 84–85, 87–88
political changes by, 80–83
Reagan and, 82–83
turmoil faced by, 88–90
Great Britain, impact of WWII
on, 14
Greece, 17
Greenglass, David, 33
Grenada, 79
Guatemala, 43–44

H
Halle, Louis, 10
Hayden, Sterling, 36
Hill, Cissie Dore, 22
Hiss, Alger, 33–34
Hitler, Adolf, 8, 9
Hollywood ten, 36
Honecker, Erich, 87
Hostage crisis, 71
House Un-American Activities
Committee (HUAC), 33–34, 36
Human rights, 68
Humphrey, Hubert, 60
Hungary, 21, 85, 87
Hussein, Saddam, 93
Hydrogen bombs, 40–41

I
Imperialism, 42
Industrial production, in
Europe, 20
Intercontinental ballistic

missiles, 41, 57, 68
Intermediate-Range Nuclear
Forces (INF) Treaty, 83, 85
Interstate Highway Act, 46–47
Interventionism, 42–44
Invasion of the Body Snatchers
(film), 46
Iran, 42–43, 71, 93
Iran-Contra affair, 78–79
Iraq, 90, 93
Iron curtain, 15
Islamic fundamentalists, 71, 91, 93

J
Japan
economic power of, 29
postwar occupation of, 25
during WWII, 10, 11
Jaruzelski, Wojciech, 77
Johnson, Lyndon, 57–60

K
Kazan, Elia, 36
Kennan, George, 16, 17–18, 38
Kennedy, John F.
assassination of, 57
Bay of Pigs and, 50, 52
Cuban Missile Crisis and, 52–54
election of, 49
on New Look, 39
Vietnam War and, 55, 57
Kennedy, Robert, 53, 60
Khomeini, Ayatollah Ruholla, 71
Khrushchev, Nikita
deposing of, 57
Kennedy and, 50, 52, 54
leadership of, 37, 42
Kim Il Sung, 28–29
Kissinger, Henry, 39, 61–64, 66
Kolb, Richard K., 58
Korean Air Lines, 78
Korean War, 28–32
Kuwait, 90

L
Lake Placid Olympics, 69
Laos, 66
Lardner, Ring Jr., 36
Laser technology, 74
Latvia, 15, 88
Lawson, John Howard, 36
LeMay, Curtis, 20, 43, 54
Lithuania, 15, 88

Lockheed U-2, 56
Long Telegram, 16
Loyalty oaths, 35

M
MacArthur, Douglas, 30, 32
Malta summit, 87–88
Maltz, Albert, 36
Mao Zedong, 25–26, 63, 64
Marshall, George C., 18
Marshall Islands, 39, 40–41
Marshall Plan, 18–20
Massive retaliation, 39, 41
Matlock, Jack F., 73
McCarthy, Joseph, 34–36
McCloy, John, 14–15
McFarlane, Robert, 78
McNamara, Robert, 54
Media, Communist takeover
  of, 17
Medvedev, Dmitri, 92
Meir, Golda, 61
Menos, Dennis, 75
Military buildup
  by China, 91
  protests against, 80
  by Soviets, 57
  U.S., 28, 32, 41, 73–76
Military spending. See Defense
  spending
Military technology, 74
Minh, Duong Van, 57
Miracle on Ice, 69
Missile targeting, 74
Mitrokhin Archive, 91
Mitrokhin, Vasili, 91
Mossadegh, Mohammad,
  42–43
Mujahedeen, 81
Muslim fundamentalists, 71,
  91, 93
Mutual assured destruction
  (MAD), 41–42, 74

N
National Aeronautics and
  Space Administration
  (NASA), 45
National Security Act, 18
National Security Council
  (NSC), 18
National Security Council
  Memorandum 68, 28, 38
Nazis, 9
New Look defense posture,
  38–39

Ngo Dinh Diem, 44
Nicaragua, 77, 78
1984 (Orwell), 46
Nitze, Paul, 27–28
Nixon, Richard
  as anti-Communist, 34, 37
  China policy of, 64–66
  defeat of, by Kennedy, 49
  election of, 60
  foreign policy of, 61–68
  reelection of, 66
  Vietnam War and, 62–63
  Watergate scandal and, 66
North Atlantic Treaty
  Organization (NATO), 21–23,
  71, 90
North Korea, 28–29, 93
North, Oliver, 78
North Vietnam, 44, 63
Nuclear arms race, 28, 40–41,
  57, 68
Nuclear proliferation, 93
Nuclear testing, 39–41, 54
Nuclear war, fear of, 45–48,
  79–80
Nuclear weapons
  buildup of, 41, 73–76
  Soviet acquisition of, 23–25
Nuclear winter, 48

O
Oil prices, 68
Olympic boycott, 70–71
On the Beach (Shute), 46
Olympics, 69
Operation Crossroads, 39
Operation Power Pack, 58
Operation Vittles, 20–21
Ornitz, Samuel, 36
Orwell, George, 46
Oswald, Lee Harvey, 57
Outpost Mission, 48

P
Pahlavi, Shah Mohammad
  Reza, 43
Peacekeeper missile, 75
Perestroika, 81
Pershing II missiles, 80
Persian Gulf War, 90, 93
Pinochet, Augusto, 62
Poindexter, John, 78
Poland, 15, 76, 77, 85, 87
Postcolonial era, 42
Postwar Europe, 10
Potsdam conference, 10–11

Powaski, Ronald E., 10, 44
Powers, Francis Gary, 56
Prados, John, 81
President, protection of, in
  nuclear attack, 48
Putin, Vladimir, 92

R
Radio Free Europe (RFE), 22
Radio Liberty (RL), 22
Reagan, Ronald
  Central America policies of,
    77–80
  foreign policy of, 72–76
  Gorbachev and, 82–83
  Iran-Contra affair and, 78–79
  Iranian hostage crisis and, 71
  during Red Scare, 35
  support of Solidarity
    movement by, 77
Red Scare, 34–36
Ridgway, Matthew, 31
Robbins, Jerome, 36
Romania, 15, 85, 87
Roosevelt, Franklin D., 9–10
Roosevelt, Kermit, 43
Rose, Lisle a., 33
Rosenberg, Ethel, 33
Rosenberg, Julius, 33
Rusk, Dean, 28
Russia, 90, 92

S
SALT. See Strategic Arms
  Limitation Talks
SALT II, 70
Sandinistas, 77
Schell, Jonathan, 80
Scott, Adrian, 36
Screen Actors Guild, 35
SDI. See Strategic Defense
  Initiative
September 11, 2001, 90–91
Shultz, George, 78
Shute, Nevil, 46
Solidarity, 77, 85, 87
South Korea, 28, 29
South Vietnam, 44, 54–55, 57,
  62–63
Soviet expansionism, 15, 16
Soviet Union
  acquisition of nuclear
    weapons by, 25
  America's view of, 32–33
  becomes nuclear power,
    23–24

China and, 63–65
dissidents in, 68
dissolution of, 90
economic problems of, 76–77, 85, 89
economic system, 8–9
fall of, 84–93
fear of nuclear war in, 79–80
goals of, 12
high point for, 72
impact of WWII on, 13–14
interventionism by, 42–44
North Korea and, 28–29
political changes in, 80–83, 88–90
Reagan's attacks on, 72–73
takeover of Eastern Europe by, 15
during WWII, 9–10
Space race, 44–45, 67
Spies, Communist, 33–34
Spillane, Mickey, 46
Sputnik, 45
Stagflation, 68
Stalin, Joseph
  death of, 37
  on German reconstruction, 15
  Mao and, 26
  testing of U.S. by, 12
  during WWII, 8–11
Star Wars, 73, 74
Stevenson, Adlai, 33, 37, 39
Strategic Air Command (SAC), 43
Strategic Arms Limitation Talks (SALT), 65
Strategic Arms Reduction Treaty (START), 87–88
Strategic Defense Initiative (SDI), 73, 74, 82
Submarine-launched ballistic missiles, 41, 57
Superbombs, 47
Syria, 93

T
Taiwan, 27, 64

Taylor, Maxwell D., 49
Teller, Edward, 40
Terrorist attacks, 90–91
Terrorist organizations, 71
Tet Offensive, 59
Tiananmen Square massacre, 86
Truman Doctrine, 17
Truman, Harry S.
  on China, 26–27
  criticism of, 27
  during Korean War, 30, 32
  on Soviets, 24
  during WWII, 10–11
Trumbo, Dalton, 36
Turkey, 17, 54

U
Ulam, Stanislaw, 40
UN Security Council, 30
Union of Soviet Socialist Republics (USSR). *See* Soviet Union
United Fruit Company, 43–44
United Nations, 10
United States
  China and, 26–27
  Communist sympathizers/spies in, 33–34
  economic system, 8
  goals of, 12
  interventionism by, 42–44
  low point for, 70–71, 72
  as major world power, 12–14
  military buildup, 28, 32
  post-war economy, 13
  as sole superpower, 90–93
  during WWII, 9–10
U.S. economy
  after Vietnam War, 68
  after WWII, 13
U.S foreign policy
  under Carter, 68, 70
  containment policy, 17–18
  flexible response doctrine, 49–50, 57
  under Kennedy, 49–50
  New Look defense posture, 38–39
  under Nixon, 61–68
  under Reagan, 72–76
  shift in, 27–28
U.S. military
  buildup of, under Reagan, 73–76
  under Bush Sr., 84
  See also Defense spending; Military buildup

V
Vance, Cyrus, 68, 70
Vanguard 1, 45
Vietcong, 54
Vietnam, 44
Vietnam War
  antiwar protests, 59–60
  disillusionment following, 61, 66, 68
  ending of, 62–63, 66
  escalation of, 54–57
  Johnson and, 57–60

W
Walesa, Lech, 76, 77
Walker, Martin, 20, 26, 32, 54, 76
Warsaw Pact, 22–23, 85
Washington-Moscow hotline, 54
Watergate scandal, 66
Welch, Joseph, 35
West Berlin, 20–21
West Germany, 21
Western Europe, 71, 80
Wilson, Charlie, 81
World War II
  deaths in, 13, 14
  impact of, 13–14
  negotiations at end of, 8–11
  world order following, 12–24

Y
Yalta conference, 9–10
Yanayev, Gennady, 89–90
Yeltsin, Boris, 89, 90
Yugoslavia, 15, 90

Picture Credits

About the Author

This is Richard Brownell's fifth title for Lucent Books. His other books include *The Fall of the Confederacy and the End of Slavery* and *America's Failure in Vietnam*, which are part of Lucent's History's Great Defeats series; *The Oklahoma City Bombing*, which is part of Lucent's Crime Scene Investigation series; and *Immigration*, part of the Hot Topics series. Richard is a published playwright with several stage productions to his credit. He also writes political commentary for various periodicals and Internet sites. He holds a bachelor of fine arts degree from New York University. Richard lives in New York City.